Trouvailles

Trouvailles

My Moments of Yūgen

SHUVASHREE CHOWDHURY

CINNAMONTEAL
DESIGN & PUBLISHING

First published in 2020 by CinnamonTeal Design & Publishing

Copyright © 2020 Shuvashree Chowdhury

ISBN: 978–93–87676–85–5

BISAC: POE000000/POETRY/General

Typesetting and Cover design: CinnamonTeal Design and Publishing

CinnamonTeal Design and Publishing
Plot No 16, Housing Board Colony
Gogol, Margao
Goa 403601 India
www.cinnamonteal.in

To Chance Encounters and Mysteries of the Universe

Author's Note

One sultry evening during the lockdown, imposed on mankind by COVID-19, when one travelled mentally rather than physically, I chanced upon two words. I not only liked the sounds of them, but they also seemed to accurately describe the nature of my travels in the recent times — physical as well as in the form of contemplation — that resulted in the lines you will read in the following pages.

Trouvaille (origin French) means a chance encounter with something wonderful, a windfall, a lucky find. Whether its stumbling across a hidden back street, discovering a quaint cafe, or connecting with a local during a journey — the joy they bring is what you call trouvaille.

Yūgen (origin Japanese) is a profound and mysterious sense of the beauty of the universe and the sad beauty of human suffering — an awareness that triggers emotional responses too deep and powerful for words.

So there, that explains the title of this book.

I like to think of myself as an explorer of life, a seeker, and a creator of flow. I believe that it is only through flow that you find a connection to your genuine self and that you then begin to live fully. Thus, I have been on a poetic journey to self-awareness and inner healing, an ongoing journey to find and connect with my true purpose and authentic self.

After years of working in demanding corporate jobs, juggling work, family and relationships, I often found myself questioning why I was doing what I was doing, wondering if there wasn't more to all of this, and if I was missing some bigger purpose. Unsettled by watching those around me live without flow, struggling to find their balance, happiness, and health, my journey as a literary fiction writer began in 2010.

Travel has been a big component of my explorations on the meaning of life — often converting to poetic expressions — in my sense of relating to my inner and outer world. Curiosity on one's self is the gateway of understanding our own sufferings and blockages that hinder us from living our truth. Inner exploration can be a deep and life-changing experience.

Through these poems, I invite readers to journey with me, to find inner connections, harmony, and flow. My goal is in creating a safe cruise for one to explore and discover one's inner peace, courage, strength, and ultimate potential. I hope to inspire and motivate people to live in a place of self-love and acceptance, thus inculcate the inner strength to never give up. In doing so, we can begin to find our inner peace while cultivating compassion in our outer interactions.

"One's destination is never a place but rather a new way of looking at things." — Henry Miller

"Don't search for the answers, which could not be given to you now, because you would not be able to live them. And the point is, to live everything. Live the questions now. Perhaps then, someday far in the future, you will gradually, without even noticing it, live your way into the answer." — Rainer Maria Rilke, Letters to a Young Poet.

A brief on my first book of poems written since 2007, that started my inward journey, is below.

Fragments is Shuvashree Chowdhury's debut collection of poetry. It is an intuitive journey into various aspects of the human experience — love, passion, jealousy, joy, spirituality, and death. The poems engage deeply with the world — turning each heartfelt moment in the hands like fragments of a broken mirror — to examine with keen intelligence, the light passing through the countless shards, towards self-realization. The poems convey insights with a perceptiveness that is at once brilliant and sumptuously lyrical, vivid, and kaleidoscopic, in a language that is elegant. The poetic journey gradually transcends into a serene, spiritually uplifting zenith — weaving its way upstream through the rocky riverbed of the spirit — the soul quivering, often crushing emotional currents.

Fifteen poems from Fragments, in a staged reading, were recited by veteran theatre artists of the reputed group — Madras Players — the oldest English language theatre group in India, in 2015 for their 60th year celebrations. The poet also read poems along with the actors. Alongside eminent international poets, she has read from her collection at important literary festivals, including 'Poetry with Prakriti' (Chennai) in 2016 at Stella Maris College, Madras Christian College, and several others. Two of the poems from this collection are also published in the Sahitya Academy anthology — 'Modern English Poetry by Younger Indians' — selected and edited by Sudeep Sen. Recital of a poem from this collection, also won her the 'Pride of India: Online Talent Hunt 2020: Winner, Poetry Competition'.

CONTENTS

AN ARTISTS RETREAT

KANCHENJUNGA

Heaven's Blue Stage

I woke up this morning to faint rays of sunlight
that pervaded my senses in anticipatory delight,
for it was accompanied by the soft chilly breeze
and a chirping of a variety of birds enticing me.

I turned to my right side — and then sat upright,
for the view from my window was as a painting:
It had splashes of colours a pallet might contain —
with a painter mixing them to get his right shade.

At the epicentre, where the colours were intense —
there emerged in the sky a smudgy ball of orange
that softly expanded with a painter's imagination,
as other colours framed his creation — in homage.

I had barely embraced the sunrise, with my senses:
stray Lhasas urging me on, with barks and whistles —
unable to drown a collective verve of chirping birds,
in urging curtains of fog to lift on a dance of clouds.

The floating white wool-clouds as they deftly danced —
dispersed now for the showstopper damsel to emerge:
her striking white silhouette glistened amid cloud girls,
as Kanchenjunga's peaks posed on Darjeeling's stage.

I stood transfixed at the poise of lofty mountain crests —
glimmering of snow with a backdrop of bronze terrain:
around them clouds danced as if elves from a fairy tale,
to sun's rays — as spotlights illuminating the blue stage.

Revitalization over a Teacup

This morning, we drove down to the Risheehat tea estate —
through 14 kilometres of winding lanes over tall mountains,
under a clear blue sky with winds bearing wild floral scents:
when on our car's windshield I heard, beheld drops of rain.

I looked out sideward through my side of the windowpane —
dark clouds had engulfed blue spans of the sky's landscape:
as they briskly filled every expanse in varied shades of grey,
then drenched us, through open windows, in dramatic rain.

We parked at the hill-entrance of a teashop lined tea estate —
it lay way below us in the valley defined by zig zag mud trails:
before we opened red-black-green Tartan printed umbrellas —
drenching our skins — the erratic Darjeeling rain pounded us.

Appraising steep stone-stairs leading to trails amid tea shrubs —
rain making the incline slushy, slippery — thus tough to walk:
we opted not to risk falling by strolling the picturesque valley,
but instead with teacups — watch rain rinse trees and shrubs.

Over cups of Darjeeling tea, senses imbued in nature's bounty —
we drove back on hill tracks — pouring rain enhancing its glory:
trudging a last stretch to rooms at the Kanchenjunga-View Walk,
I rushed to open the windows — to grab fistfuls of magnificence.

Rain with biting winds we braced — made us crave for tea again
but the water took much longer to boil even in an electric kettle:
I infused teabags as I glanced out, awaiting to relish hill flavours —
but my soul thumped with the brilliance of a rainbow in the sky!

Leaving my teacup — I hastened to gather a heartful of sunshine,
as I had not seen a rainbow etched so visibly in a fairly long time:
it stretched across the sky's blue canvas, over a backdrop of hills —
its dazzling green infused in me renewed vitality and confidence.

   Shuvashree Chowdhury

The Kanchenjunga-View Walk

The rainclouds, they floated up so amazingly slow,
they wrapped the pine trees in their spooky course,
while sun now gleamed through thickset mangroves —
or was it, auburn glow of strands flying off charcoal?

Amidst the steep avenues — while I leisurely strolled,
the Kanchenjunga's peaks shone white in sun's glow
and even though I felt the chill deep inside my bones —
it was at the glimpse of her face I undoubtedly froze.

Squatting on a pavement she fanned an iron brazier —
on which several cobs of corn roasted golden-black:
her fair face now beet-red glistened in its warm glow,
or was it the colour of self-assuredness she radiated!

It was as if a halo she wore over her — as of a goddess,
in life's fight armed in optimism, dignity, compassion:
I walked towards her drawn by her pretty warm smile
on her wine-red lips and sparkling slanted brown eyes.

I noticed thick red vermillion on a parting of her head —
as in his school-uniform — her boy playfully grimaced:
even as I awaited my ear of corn to roast to satisfaction,
another face, as if the moon rising over hills, drifted up.

She smiled at the squatting corn-lady, antics of her child;
their eyes crinkling ravines-deep, faces looked delighted:
Bent to retain her balance, the woman's silver hair shone —
as clouds riding white mountain peaks — she approached.

Strapped from her forehead, behind her a coir rope tarried,
it held a white tote baggage, also two black stroller suitcases:
behind her mountainous bulk strode a young spirited couple —
on their way to their honeymoon — at a cosy hill-view hotel.

In awed compassion I strolled munching kernels of corncob,
to catch a glimpse of two women emerging through thick fog:
Jute baskets hung from coir ropes, behind their chatting heads —
of a tough day's work, of rigid supervisors they reckoned with.

A third iron canopied haunt I walked to, past two similar ones —
Darjeeling's youth congregate at this Kanchenjunga-View Walk:
on dates — over tea, coffee, corn, peanuts, Maggi, not much else,
livening a cloudy landscape with a fashion-sense par excellence.

I walk on munching roasted peanuts as fog shrouds me or clouds —
shivering, I dash to a tin roof shed, of a wool garment seller's cart:
she smiles, bids me to sit — glowing from compassion not makeup,
as thunder roars, rain whips, I'm sheathed in resilience of hill folk.

   Shuvashree Chowdhury

Finding our Happy Space

"Where does the rainbow end / in your soul or on the horizon?"
           — Pablo Neruda.

Each one of us,
has within us — a place,
even if it seems
barely residual at times,
and we have to look for it
deep inside our soul —
a spot where there's joy.

If we find that source of light,
then dwell on it — it will burn
the darkness of pain
we've nurtured,
and allowed to flourish —
by disseminating it to those
we encounter or deal with.

The rainbow of joy we paint,
with egoless humility —
will not only light up our lives,
but of those who step
into our Happy Space:
They will return,
seeking that sunshine
even in rainy days,
to thus fill our life
with renewed love —
taking away loneliness if any.

It is our positive thinking,
and actions — that brings
the lamp of happiness
into our hearts — so we may
hold up its glow to eradicate
the ever-increasing hate,
and darkness of intolerance
to light up the world.

                    Shuvashree Chowdhury

Sunrise on the Valley

I'm looking out of the window of this heritage house,
sitting on a king-sized bed flanked by its three windows —
on my left, the sight of the palace's square lawn-garden,
in front, a view of soft peaks and valleys of Kalimpong.

Swathed in the soft sunlight, birds chirping to my right,
I focus on green peaks over the front porch and drive —
that's lined by gladioli, dahlias, gerberas — till the lawn,
where blue, white, red and yellow Buddhist flags swirl.

Stray dogs are still, quiet, and there's no man in sight
as sun leisurely traces the low roofs against hill sides —
in view past tender-green tartan curtains of our room,
swinging in the chilly breeze — aside white lace drapes.

I've just watched the sun creep up hills and valleys far,
darkness gently opening its core like a dark rose bud:
magically blooming into a white rose to stir the world —
another night giving birth to a new day draped in hope.

My Love affair with Teesta

She spreads her legs wide to mother — India's eastern region,
from her emanates — love, empathy, unrestrained compassion.
But she can also be tough, and will drown you in her currents —
if you attempt to bathe, to dowse in her your unrestrained lust.

An essence of raw beauty — hilltops see her in embryonic pose,
in valleys, lying on her sides as if figurine of a damsel in bronze;
from bridges she's on her bridal bed, lined by a variety of petals —
like jasmine — strings of waterfalls trickle her black-rock tresses.

As you drive up, your sights touch her enticing green silhouette,
she gently opens her legs wide — to embrace you into her realm:
lost in the scents of her long silken tresses blowing on your face —
her white-stone lined banks keep you falling in without caution.

This morning after breakfast, we left Park Hotel in Kalimpong —
to get a glimpse of Teesta — after a downward drive for an hour:
her lean upper torso we had traversed driving in from Darjeeling,
as wrapping her hips in a sarong she's wearing, is a yellow bridge.

My love affair with river Teesta began when I was a girl of five —
driving up her verges with my parents, to St. Joseph's Convent:
crying to be in her arms, every night after dorm lights went out,
to dream she'd carry me in her arms, reach me home by dawn.

BANARAS

A Spiritual Dance Recital

After an early shower this morning,
I sped out to the streets of Banaras:
it was past six-thirty in late February,
and I'd miss the most charming part.

It was a hurried walk from my hotel
to the famed Dashashwamedh Ghat;
past the Vishwanath temple's campus —
already at the task of setting up stalls.

Florists had barely set up the displays —
and tea stalls their kettles just warmed:
A chain of beggars had already flanked
this stretch — both hands outstretched.

The ghat by now was set up for act one,
a glow of dawn raising its azure curtain:
Naga sadhus on stage ready to perform
for Ganges, past the line of saffron flags.

Throngs of people waded into the river,
bathing in obeisance to rising Sun god:
Sandal anointed pundits, after holy dips —
waited under canopies to initiate rituals.

Barbers performing on stage this long,
first to start the nimble-fingered dance —
of eyes, hand movements as if Kathak:
the patrons rivetted to facial expression.

Soul aloof — I stand in the amphitheatre
viewing this dance-drama in curious awe:
swathed in a *vilambit* (slow) *laya* and *taal* —
I'm led within, into my soul's dancefloor.

Serpent around Shiva's Neck

The series of little shops slowly waking up to life,
flanked this slender lane, we'd just wandered into —
as serpent like, it wound as if around Shiva's neck,
all the way up — till the four entrances of his shrine.
They sold Banarasi silk saris, make-up, ornaments;
stone idols, wooden toys, flowers and steel-utensils;
kumkum, sandal paste and fruits both dry and fresh,
also incense sticks and all conceivable puja elements —
for a devout trip to famed Kashi Vishwanath temple.

Amid the shops, revered cows authoritatively roved,
thrusting heads in miniscule iron grill-gated lodgings:
As fed by residing temple priests, out of steel buckets —
in starting their day out thus, who believed it is sacred.
The arterial road that Vishwanath Galli branches from,
is the busiest and most commercial stretch of Banaras:
Gowdalia Chowk, Gyanvapi to Dashashwamedh Ghat —
where with flourish Ganga *arati* is currently conducted,
all rituals of birth, life, death — from times immemorial.

It was over a walk to this ghat that we'd taken a deviation
to stroll in Vishwanath Galli — coming to life at eight am;
with no plan or inclination, to join throngs to the temple —
for at nine, with a friend we had a breakfast appointment.
But as sequence of shopkeepers intoned encouragements —
'This Saturday, queues to the shrine are light' they stated,
'So if you hurry, with luck you'll have a peaceful darshan.'
The shopkeepers obviously had a sharp business acumen,
for a fee we deposited our mobiles, shoes, bags, valuables —
and collected a set of locker keys with pre-set puja baskets:
adhering to stern restrictions inside Kashi temple's premises,
for security reasons — to check threats from devious elements
that in management and pilgrims — a sense of security eluded.

                              Shuvashree Chowdhury

After an hour of us walking bare feet with serpentine queues,
we were relieved to be entering the temples exterior premises —
but to our immense disillusionment, also to our exasperation,
the queue from here on only got more taut like Shiva's mane —
for we now zigzagged on a rectangular patch through steel rails,
just after we had crossed Gyanvapi mosque — Aurangzeb built
after demolishing the original Kashi temple — in his conquests.
Though, the Shivling remains the primary religious attraction
after it was saved by the key priest — in ducking it into the well
that now lies fortified in a forty pillared low-roofed colonnade,
and still stands testimony to the grave chronological upheaval.
As queen Ahilyabai in its current form later rebuilt the temple —
inside there's a seven feet high stone statue of Nandi the bull,
gifted by Raja of Nepal, now adjacent to the east of the arcade.

Standing in queue amid Kashi temple and Gyanvapi mosque —
both heavily guarded by an army task force around the clock,
most pilgrims — especially the ladies, burst out singing bhajans
in the name of Shiva — inspiring themselves into his presence.
Numerous monkeys here, prance to rhythms of these hymns —
as they swing gaily around trees and steel bars in red bottoms,
their pint-sized babies bending low — deftly drinking from taps
from which you may quench your thirst now and fill your urns
if you haven't brought water from the Ganges for the worship:
to pour over the Shivling to appease the Lord, more your soul —
along with milk sprinkled with rose petals — sold in paper cups,
handed out deftly by temple staff, from out of an Amul caravan.

After a two hour queue, in February — with the weather still cool,
I find myself inadvertently shoved — into the attendance of Shiva;
but before I have the presence of mind to offer milk I've brought —
as in the jostle I've been shoved into a podium with several altars,
also doors and windows ushering in steams of astounding sunlight —
then I just about manage to pour the milk over the pious Shivling:
I'm curtly indicated the way out and urged to step out of the door,
without a minute to rest my weary mind, at the shrine of the lord.

I'm walking back to gate number four — with my mind in a furore
and my heart disappointed at this momentous — perfunctory tour,
when to my left I see an engraved door, past whose porch an altar
I am enthused to find — as I may rest my fasting and seeking mind.
As it leads to Parvati or Annapurna — the goddess of nourishment,
in whose sanctuary I can pray unobstructed by the pushing crowds —
intent on drowning the Shivling in milk only to appease their souls:
while just like Parvati — I prefer to feed the starving with a purpose.
Then I feel I've been brought to Annapurna by divine intervention —
in craving a spiritual experience — dissatisfied with ritual excursion;
so I may go back to my work, and spread intellectual nourishment,
to thus be blessed with a meaningful life in harmony with my vision.

The Sounds of Death

The bells clanged urgently — piercingly loud,
the brass drums reverberated wild;
as the priest stood on one foot at a time —
flailing his tiny *arati* — with no reprieve.

The little temple was so full of fumes
that threatened to blind my sight,
but they weren't all from the incense stand:
there were several pyres burning outside.

As the clamour of drums accelerated
and brass bells jangled with insistence and might,
the priest hopped over to shove wood from pyres
into a pit, to chase away spirits — to my right.

The four men ringing bells — as if death knells,
also women wriggling ten *dumroos* with might —
were unaffected by their handiwork in a cubby,
but as about to rupture — my eardrums thumped.

Few visited this temple — other than crematorium staff,
including a few westerners who frequented its enclave —
with no idea of Hindu death rituals and superstitions,
that made outcasts of the dead and families it swathed.

Those tourists who came by, tended to return often —
as they began to gravitate to these deafening sounds
that wrapped them in a trance-like hypnotic state:
'Gets rid of negative energies', they addictively claimed!

Inside, was an altar — led down by a short flight of stairs,
that the stone Shivling under a tripod — was fortified in:
where the priest chanted on one leg, flailing his *arati* —
as fires from pyres outside — blew high above the grills.

I watched these fires rise, as orange balloons at night —
as if lifting souls off their pyres — that burned bright:
while on the right wall an appeased Kali, painted all blue —
skipped gaily with her head thrown back, the tongue out.

I remained rooted, taking deep breaths, my eyes sealed —
no way I'd leave — succumbing to deadly discordant sounds,
that perhaps disperse souls from Banaras — never to be reborn:
in thus attaining Moksh — at the famed Manikarnika Ghat.

                    Shuvashree Chowdhury

The Naked Holy Men

I stare at you with glassy eyes, over a haze of my chillum,
to brandish my feather broom on you as you pass by —
whether or not you care to bow in seeking my blessings,
or let me apply on your forehead — a pinch of my ash.

Don't be repulsed by my earliest homo-sapiens look
that I've imbibed from living in the hills and woods:
I'm now creatively adorned, to project a distinctive look —
with rudraksh beads, flowers, artefacts, trident and sword.

My nudity is no concern of mine, then why make it yours?
my yoga-fit body with mud and ash I anoint in heat or cold —
to remind me that in dedication to Shiva — my life is renounced:
would I then, for my long matted-hair — crave your opinion?

I squat or crouch, sleep bare on the cold banks of the Ganges now;
alms I'm allowed, I cook in earthen pots — on charcoal kilns I mount:
At Banaras, I've halted only in transiting from Khumb Mela at Prayag —
dwelling in seclusion of the Himalayas long — from civilization I recoil.

At the early age of sixteen I denounced the regular life you live,
all connections — family, friends, even society I vehemently perished:
Yet killing my youthful male libido, was my most challenging sacrifice —
that my *akhara* beat out of my phallus to attest my spiritual incline.

I now live on an extended new life after my *pind daan* and *shradh* —
my personal death rituals I've conducted, to validate total renunciation:
only then was I inducted with my *guru mantra* after six rigorous years,
another ten to prove myself; so that at 32 — a Naga Sadhu I was reborn.

You think my life is regressive, as it's impossible for you to envision
a make belief ascetic world — eating, sleeping, existing without purpose:
but I dread duties, pain, and strife you juggle, of mistrust, jealousy, hate —
trivial rivalry above all else; to die and turn like me to mud or ash!

Serving Shiva

I stand at the Assi Chowraha in Banaras
with my vendor's open cart;
equipped with a cylinder of LPG gas
and a stove over which stands —
an iron *karhai* with steaming cooking oil,
also a square wooden board and staff
to roll out the *puris* I serve.

I also have some vessels on my cart —
in one I store the damp-cloth wrapped *puri* dough,
another holds the rose flavoured sweet syrup —
into which the piping hot jalebis I ladle out.
Then there's a big basin of the *subzi* —
of potato and peas in thick gravy,
with liberal dashes of soya beans and paneer:
as I believe, breakfast is the most important meal —
that with utmost care — I serve in paper bowls
with the four pieces of *puri* per paper plate.

You cannot miss my presence at this *chowk*,
along with my friend who assists my work —
I'm here from eight in the morning till after noon,
always wearing my Chennai-checks apron:
After a compulsory, sacred Ganges bath —
having applied sandal paste on my forehead.

My skills at my work I've honed with my father —
who at Kachowari Gali Chowk had his setup;
on whose demise I set up this cart
I nurture and serve at, with all my heart —
which people of the locality reciprocate,
and passers-by tend to stop, taste and promulgate —
on seeing patrons seated with their plates at doorsteps.

                    Shuvashree Chowdhury

This morning when you first passed me by,
I noticed you hesitated to stop and try —
the first batch of my puffed *puris* and *jalebis*
peeking out of the vessels they were contained in;
even as a few people had started to stand around
for their helping of traditional Banarasi food.

But after a walk of our neighbourhood — you returned,
though street food — isn't your preferred patronal:
With my warm smile and gracious encouragement,
you hesitantly took a seat at a nearby doorstep —
on which I'd spread plastic runners for my clients.

After a plate of four *puris*, you savoured two *jalebis* —
its rose essence stirred sweet syrup carrying you to heaven:
On seeing your face glowing with a deep satisfaction,
I offered to get you yogurt from the opposite *lassi* shop —
with it, like us Banarasi's — you relished many more *jalebis*.

Much to my pleasure, and deep pride in my occupation —
you asked me during a brief and casual conversation,
'What do you do Raja — once you close this shop'?
'I go home after noon', he cheerily blurted,
'As I have to be early at the evening's *arati* at the Assi Ghat —
for there I play the *dumroo* — that's closest to my heart'.

You ascribed my goodness to my sensitivity and warmth,
to the smile that never fades serving clients — even in a rush,
and to the passion I have for my simple mundane job —
yet for free I play the *dumroo* at the lucrative hours for my shop.
As money doesn't enrich one's life as dedication to a heartfelt cause —
my entire life is devoted to Shiva — my one and only Lord:
but merely drowning his head with milk doesn't appease my soul —
as it's through serving humanity that I actually serve my inner God!

Pappu's Chai Shop

We first walked past this tea shop on our morning walk,
after a boat ride that brought us to the famed Assi Ghat:
where we had tall glasses of lemon tea — also fruit salad,
at a café with a wide view of the Ganges across its garden.

Laid on the *chowrasta* this chaiwala's benches were vacant,
while he sat at his usual podium to the right of the entrance:
Overseeing vegetable vendors — setting up shop on the road,
we headed on to a *puri* vendor's stall in quest for breakfast.

Sated with *puri-subzi*, and jalebi — we strolled to Pappu's shop,
its interior benches now filled up with regular and local patrons —
holding open newspapers over which their sights were engaged
in passionate debates — about culture, politics and social welfare.

These elders — teachers, professors, and newspaper journalists,
also comprising of the literary who's who of the city of Benaras:
were the elites who now congregated here, and were upholders —
of Benarasi culture — tending to now bear the strain of tourism.

Taking our seats on the benches laid symmetrically on the road,
we were served tall glasses of the chai — that is most regular here:
which to my disappointment was not near the best I had in Kashi —
let alone meeting my expectations of this reputed shop of Banaras.

But Manoj, learning we'd come seeking his father's signature tea,
requested us to wait a while, so that we might carry away his legacy
that's served to the Hindi novelist Kashi Singh, and literary friends:
A glass of black tea, with liberal dashes of ginger and lemon slices.

A second glass of tea — served with care, was distinct and superior,
reviving my faith in visiting an eatery popularised by common taste;
but it was the crowd at Raja's *puri* shop that stared at me in the face —
how his attitude of *seva* (service) stood tall to complacency and fame.

                    Shuvashree Chowdhury

The Loss of Heritage

After breakfast at the popular Korean café —
in a narrow lane parallel to the river Ganges,
we were strolling the busy network of alleys
flanked by little shops — of fervent sales' people:
fathers, or mothers, with their teenaged sons —
who knew how to grab your attention,
and engage you with astute business acumen —
to sundry merchandises — of metal handiwork;
incense, aromatic oils; also jewellery and garments
that are stylishly crafted and deftly woven
for customers — of foreign origin.

Niftily dodging cows in this holy terrain
at Bengali tola's narrow crisscrossing lanes —
exploring with a curiosity led by my Bengali origin,
we were roaming with an American author friend —
who had introduced us to the well-known Bona Café —
where we had tall glasses of lemon, ginger and honey tea
with sandwiches, French fries, and sautéed vegetables —
out of a menu of continental and Korean options.

After a stopover at Lahiri Mahashay's ashram —
it was in search of his old house with Ma Durga's temple,
that we crossed the invisible yet pertinent line of religion.
The young Hindu shopkeeper whom we asked the way,
considered his responsibility to signal and mention to us —
'Beyond that house, it's Muslim dominated'.
This didn't inhibit us to stop by shop-cum-residences,
to converse with craftsmen in Muslim sections —
living for generations in houses interwoven with Hindus,
to flourish in embroidering saris and salwar-suits
designed to be exported to other states and nations —
the surplus produce more than ample for the local market.

As we strode raptly to the old family house in Benaras —
of the harbinger of Kriya yoga — now world prominent,
I heard the droning jangle of running machinery —
from behind several closed doors — that were wooden.
While others randomly stopped — to converse with locals,
I shoved open and looked past one raucous door, with caution.
Several machines, whizzed in elongated rooms flanking an alley
that led into the darkness of the portico of the Muslim residence.
Only one man in each hall — wearing *lungi-kurta* with skull cap,
worked on operating three to four looms in succession.

Power looms with their high capacity for production —
had deemed extinct — the work of artisans,
who had spun handlooms for several generations,
but had to abandon ancestral skills of finesse and specialization —
to be relegated to a life of poverty in losing their heritage:
To commence power looms themselves or work for rich owners —
who had scant respect for their talent and for rareness of hand woven,
so to aid mass production, killed legacy, for commercial expansions.

               Shuvashree Chowdhury

Ashes

Fire around me everywhere,
the heat intolerable to bear
and yet I cannot feel a thing,
my soul has lost its ability to care.

Covered in ashes from head to toe,
the numerous fires spurting more —
I stand amidst death drenched in rain,
wondering if this is what I live for!

Ashes over me I cannot distinguish —
which is human, which of material thing?
Human or wooden, ashes are the same:
to turn to ashes then — a lifetime I live!

The drizzle now turns to a heavy shower
drenching my being to the very core,
yet on these fires they have no power —
roaring high over the pyres they've lit.

Below the river Ganges peacefully flows,
washing away ashes the fires have restored;
men are hurrying around me everywhere —
with corpses, guts — for which fires don't care!

Wasn't it this afternoon that I saw her face —
peaceful and calm in death's embrace:
when bathing and dressing her like a bride,
grooming her well for the final goodbye.

The narrow, winding lanes as I traversed —
I knew what lay at the end of these paths,
yet I wasn't ready to face the ultimate truth:
My life — is mere ash on the pyre in death!

As I now stand sombrely watching her pyre lit,
my heart is numb from all the sights it hit;
my face, eyes, smarting from the thick smoke —
are red — incapable of insulating as my soul.

The Manikarnika Ghat in Banaras, they say
is the holiest crematorium for Hindus till date —
it frees one from the cycle of Life and Death:
Has given me Moksha from the fear of Death!

  Shuvashree Chowdhury

The Eternal Fire

That evening at eight —
we walked the narrow trail
via the river path,
that led to the Manikarnika Ghat.
Serenading us was a chilly breeze
as we doubled our speed —
once the burning pyres were visible.

There were several men and women,
mostly of foreign origin
the rest staff from the crematorium,
who intently watched the proceedings —
as though a game of cavorting at a circus,
with men transporting logs — to blaze fire-rings.
Viewers squatted or stood on their toes
alongside the cows and buffaloes —
who had the relaxed ringside view here,
interspaced with local dogs who were rare
but nevertheless — always present there.

We crossed a large iron scale —
standing tall by piles of logs they weighed,
that aided abundant and brisk busines —
as for every pyre that was lit,
a minimum of 350 kgs of wood was required —
to ensure the human body was desiccated
with no trace of a lifetime's existence —
to a mere handful of ashes,
whose material source is indistinguishable.
To then be immersed into the Ganges below —
so the soul may be relieved from the tedious cycle
of several births and deaths — that is otherwise inevitable,
to the furore of attaining the much sought-after Moksha —
thus will never be born once more, to this worlds afflictions.

In the chilly breeze — we moved up close to the smoke,
feeling the sweltering heat of the fires below —
taking the stairs, to meet two men who sat in the galleries:
manoeuvring the relentless circus of death at their stadium,
from where they kept the weighing scale in their vision —
to supervise the customary commercial practice
of allowing the pyre bearers to be the one to decide —
to what extent they would allow their deceased to incinerate,
if they couldn't afford more wood to char the full human form.

Moreover, if you're in a hurry to leave the crematorium —
have a train or flight to board — to go back to your life once more,
or simply cannot afford — or will not consider wasting wood:
you could request that the unburned parts of your kin —
usually comprising the last to burn — female hips,
along with the human naval and the intestines;
also the sturdy chest bones of the male skeleton,
remain unburned — to be finally beaten down with force
so you may carry broken bones to a holier bay or confluence —
or have these parts immersed in the Ganges with the ashes.

One of the two men — now overseeing this venture of death,
willingly encouraged us into a prolonged conversation —
for how many people — even if writers, photographers, or artists,
whether it be — of Indian or even of foreign origin;
more so, a Hindu woman as myself —
care to find out what truly happens in this arena of death —
especially behind the scenes of even this famed crematorium:
So he eagerly takes us to the inheritors of this pageant of transience.

Cremation in Banaras is an age-old family run business —
operated by extended families over several generations,
such that each of four real brothers and their cousins
along with extended families of each generation —
all own and run the Manikarnika Ghat crematorium.
In ten-day turns, each brother resides here twenty-four hours,
to have their next turn come up every twenty days —

     Shuvashree Chowdhury

till when they go back to living with their families
who live normal lives — no fuss they are sustained by death!
The twenty days of not working are a crucial reprieve —
away from the constant drone here of *hari bol*
such that even in their sleep day and the night —
they hear chants in the name of the lord as mere humdrum.

Hari bol (chant the name of the lord) — from times immemorial
is a spiritual connect — between the Hindu living and the dead;
a fine line — in passing over to the next world,
till turned to ashes with the hope to never again be born:
As to be cremated at this revered Manikarnika Ghat,
assures you — that you've completed the seven cycles of birth
and thereby with several lives — you're forever done!

There's an eternal fire of death, next to the master of ceremonies,
on a piece of firewood at the altar by the first-floor windowsill —
and every pyre brought to Manikarnika is lit only out of this kiln
that has a distinct view of the row boats down by the Ganges:
You can avail to go far out midstream — to immerse the ashes
of your deceased kin — into the holy flow that washes away all sin.

At the Carnival

I stood in awe of the mystically elegant Ganges,
on stone steps leading to Dashashwamedh Ghat —
she flowed unperturbed by immense veneration,
with orchestrated sights, sounds ushering sunset.

Her soft waves caught the glow of flickering lights
dotting Varanasi's ghats — yet she gently cascaded,
detached to the incense, sandalwood, and flowers —
with a synchronised flailing of layered brass lamps.

Throngs gathered by the ramp to watch the show,
that every evening — placed Ganga on the catwalk:
As propelling her delicate steps *bhajans* were sung —
with *dumroos* keeping rhythm as if *tabla* to her *taal.*

Broad chested men, strikingly agile as super models
in *akhara*-fit bodies chiselled with yogic persistence:
deftly flailing the brass *aratis* they held with devotion —
to Ganga's movements as if of a showstopper model.

Viewers from all over the world jostled in this crowd,
as midstream — boats full of people watched close-up:
all intricacies of Ganga's form showcased in devotion —
as from side-wings or backstage of the spring carnival.

With her poise, Ganga was an epitome of femininity,
not losing her reserved elegance even in heroic glory:
she generously gives of herself in her loving empathy,
even to those who pollute but worship her as divinity.

Every woman can flow with compassionate empathy,
upon cleansing her soul of the refuses of a tough life:
as she also has the strength to withstand being defiled —
in nurturing her soul in service to God and mankind.

    Shuvashree Chowdhury

Life's Direction

After sunrise painted the daybreak skies of Banaras,
with strokes of the master painter's brush on canvas:
blue sky came alive; orange lighting a wide spectrum —
as canopying the rising of civilization by the Ganges.

Ghats now readying for the day's business of religion
drove me to take sanctuary in a boat ride on Ganges —
to rest my mind in her lap so I may detach from life,
open my heart up to divinity, nurture a spiritual side.

A young boatman — on my strolls of the promenade,
trailing me with a desolate look I could not override —
urging me to take his first ride to savour the sunrise;
to swathe my soul in harmony wafting in the Ganges.

The soft golden sunlight playing with all my senses,
a chilly wind caressing my hair, stirring a river smell
into alerting my mind and skin to feel the existence —
of the omnipotent force guiding my life's direction.

Where its Purest

Across the river, a young man took us at seven thirty,
well after the sun had risen sensuously and artistically —
from Dashashwamedh Ghat, bastion of pious activity,
rowing with forces of Sun and Ganges, his frame wiry.

With high currents midstream we crossed a motorboat,
of westerners — who couldn't help clicking every instant
of the unique architectural beauty of heritage structures
lining ghats we left behind — names depicting their pasts.

The receding edifices of each ghat had distinctive charm,
as many were palaces of Maratha Royals, or of rich clans —
who visited the holy city of Banaras often, to pay homage
at Vishwanath temple — with a few sacred dips in Ganges.

At these ghats body builders postured in front of *akharas*,
chiselled men in challenging yoga mudras — faced the sun:
with blessings of Ganges, posed atop stoic stone pedestals —
Naga Sadhus set about their chores as if on theatre stages.

After we had crossed a speed boat of enthusiastic tourists —
who speaking Tamil, observed all as if memorizing digits:
our boatman anchored beside bathers on the furthest side,
so we got views of Banaras from behind its mirrored sights.

After *chai* at a stall, along with people changing their clothes —
in completing mass holy dips at secluded ghats, so aren't shy:
we set forth on the boat to diagonally cross back, to Assi Ghat —
also prominent among the famed ghats of the city of Banaras.

The boat trip was more challenging this time, against the tide —
propelling the boatman to use all his boyish might on the ride:
We filled up bottles of holy water midstream where its purest,
noting — sublime joy, triumph, is found at the peak of distress.

　　　　　Shuvashree Chowdhury

A Purposeful Literary Life

On the stage of the classroom you stood —
addressing the aficionados of literature,
who've been invited to pay their homage
to the well-known departed Hindi litterateur:
along with professors and batches of students
who shared with him their Alma Mater —
the Udai Pratap Autonomous College,
where we're all now solemnly gathered —
after you brought us to listen to your tribute,
as you're being profiled in this book, on Banaras.

The deceased was your senior, friend and mentor;
also as you're a friend of Kashinath Singh — his brother:
Gaya Singh — yourself a reputed Hindi professor,
who's revered in this city that pride's it's men of letters —
also, that you're a strong upholder of Banaras's culture;
thus have been called upon with other literary stalwarts
to speak at this afternoon's bereavement get-together —
of those the Hindi language scholastically nurtured.

As an essayist, poet, and a short-fiction writer,
also a literary critic, linguist, and commentator —
the late Namvar Singh has had a progressive career:
A long-term academician — as founder and chairman,
of the Delhi based Jawaharlal Nehru University —
at the Centre of Indian Languages; also a professor
in several reputed colleges of Hindi literature,
including Banaras Hindu University —
where he completed and received his doctorate.
This after matriculation and higher secondary education —
from this college where we're now assembled,
to pay venerations — reacquaint with the departed soul's
magnanimous contribution to nationalist literature —
for which he received the Sahitya Academi Award.

The attentive audience seemed amply morose,
even as the speakers droned in monotonous tones —
keeping their voices and sights bent low
in reviving memories of interfaces with the deceased.
For didn't he also belong to them as he did to Banaras —
even though in Delhi his remains still await to be cremated!
A posthumous honour in this college, he's accorded —
for as its illustrious scholar he's brought upon it credit,
that will inspire batches of students currently tutored:
who'll take today's participation back with them,
and never fail to evoke — hard work pays rich dividends,
not just in this lifetime, but also after one's death.

In recognizing that life opens many more doors —
in one's childhood and throughout youth,
that start to narrow beyond one's age of twenty-two:
students may be inspired to create a vision for their life,
which they can feel free to update from time to time;
to also pursue short term goals and desires
so their cruise of life may be more substantial.
Long-term goals need patience, and steadfast purpose —
for only with a sustained body of recognizable work
and not just bursts of fading out streaks of genius,
by large shooting stars that fall leaving fleeting trails:
Can you earn the devotion — not only of your patrons,
but also contend to be the pride of mere acquaintances.

          Shuvashree Chowdhury

Enjoying every Moment

A tour we took, of the Ashoka Pillar, Thai temple, Stupa at Sarnath —
to this itinerary we added Banaras Hindu University's campus,
also its newly built Vishwanath temple that students frequent:
then reached Assi Ghat just after the regular *arati* had commenced.

Several young women rushed towards us as a swarm of locusts —
buzzing around, making us buy their last few leaf-boat *diyas*
that are tiny candles, lit and drifted along with flowers and incense —
by those seeking to float a solemn wish, or purely in reverence.

After our offerings to Ganges, we hired a motorboat for a long ride —
which would be tough on a rowboat in high tide, at this late time:
to go past the famed ghats lining Banaras, ending at its last ornate one —
on a canvas of dark balmy sky, each delicately lit edifice creating a collage.

Glittering silhouettes of ghats — distinctive in architectural tradition,
breezed by, as if in a film representation of diverse Indian states:
as ghats were built by maharajas and affluent, in front of their palaces —
titles extolled on the horizon — as if images of national integration.

A jarring motor sound upsetting tranquility, and barring conversation;
over that, insects hounded us — attacking our faces, necks and hands:
yet they couldn't diminish the exquisiteness and bliss of these moments,
as I tend to focus on relishing flashes in time — despite life's deterrents.

A Feast of Lights

I walked in the direction of an impending sunrise,
from Gowdali chowk down to Daswasmedha Ghat;
past the Vishwanath Gali's entrance beginning life —
way before the rest of an ascending eastern world.

Flower sellers tried to waiver my steady attention,
even as I hastened to celebrate in a feast of lights;
while the beggars flanking this path since dawn,
tried to steal my mind's eye from a diffident sun.

My vision dodged arched frames, flags, canopies
to detect a grey sky — burst into streams of light
which grew so intense, as I watched their gleam,
till they erupted into fissures of tangerine delight.

Orange streaks of light spread diffusing grey sky,
as rituals of custom, religion, picked momentum;
past unflappable orange flags on pole lined ghats
the fleets of boats stood guard — as Sun emerged.

Sun now decked up in silver lined orange turban —
his bridegroom's face glorious with a silken halo:
his lovelorn face took on a tangerine hued glow
in lifting princess Ganga's dark azure sari's hood.

An orange feast of light announced to this world
that the royals, Sun and Ganges are both wedded:
as men and women bowed to priests in ceremony —
hailing the couple, partaking of love's visual buffet.

 Shuvashree Chowdhury

Aimless in Banaras

At the launch of the book 'Aimless in Banaras',
we had gathered by Pizzeria Café on Assi Ghat —
at the venue, it is 'Kashi Annapurna Bookhouse'
with a broad view from its windows — of Ganges.

A cool breeze swathing us — fanned anticipation
as trays of chai were passed around in clay cups:
I sat on a floor rug, facing the two wide windows —
listening to conversations floating around galore.

Literary stalwarts of Banaras gathered here now —
in addition to chief guests who faced us on sofas:
We start an hour late waiting for Kashinath Singh —
who at eighty-three, is ailing yet making the effort.

Special guests — journalists, novelists, poets, critics;
those who often meet at nearby Pappu's chai shop
to discourse local flavours, culture, heritage, politics,
featured in Bishwanath Ghosh's 'Aimless in Banaras'.

Literary critic Chauthi Ram Yadav initiated dialogue,
as he introduced, reviewed locations and characters —
several of whom were seated here for this meeting:
stirring a reminiscent old-worldly charm now fading.

Kashinath Singh, who's a writer and scholar of Hindi,
is distinguished for writing Hindi novels, short stories —
was a professor of Hindi at Banaras Hindu University;
received the Kendra Sahitya Akademi Award, in 2001.

As one of the best chroniclers of this city of Banaras,
also known for his novel *Kashi Ka Assi* — now a film:
is much revered by guests assembled for this chronicle —
asserted this book depicts the true essence of Banaras.

Dr. Gaya Singh a professor, a distinguished Banarasi,
made an impassioned address on his book-character —
rendering his daughter, the event's anchor speechless:
as she saluted him, calling forth — Dr. Ramdeo Singh.

Several others featured in the book shared experiences —
among them a medical doctor, pen seller and professor:
additional audiences on loudspeakers outside the venue,
along with the Assi Ghat *arati*, lent the book a divine air.

     Shuvashree Chowdhury

An Epiphany

Today, I am in the mood for a distinctive sunrise —
in Banaras, sun's varied facets appear at every turn:
so I stroll from Daswasmedha to Darbhanga Ghat,
dodging persistent boatmen and determined priests.

In front of Brij Rama Palace I find an isolated spot —
on a parapet atop a series of steps from the Ganges:
I seek a panoramic view of the sunrise over the ghat —
as the birds start their synchronised dance in chorus.

In front, a red iron temple stands upholding a trident,
inside which rest cosy — six tiny black stone Shivlings,
each anointed in ash and garlanded with fresh flowers —
seated on a square slab with sides delineated in 'OM'.

A line of row boats stoically queued up in attendance,
as if to link pilgrims from this temple — to the horizon
that's now a grey stretch dividing sky from the Ganges —
both brush-stroked in the pre-sunrise gold and orange.

The sky now bursts into light — as in a floodlit stadium,
from which the yellow, tangerine backdrop withdraws —
with golden flashes of light enthralling my mind's eye,
instilling spirituality and a self-assurance I may live by.

An orange ball emerges on horizon's grey sari's folds —
a child cradled in earth's lap — raising its monk's head,
to convey — I came into this world alone, as I'll depart:
in ordinating my *vairagi* soul in an epiphany of rebirth.

Looking Back on Life

The boatman looked at me with a glint of surprise —
then eclipsed it up with a shy heart-warming smile,
as alone I got into his boat at Daswasmedha Ghat
after bargaining for a solitary cruise of the Ganges.

After delighting in a mid-March sunrise from ashore —
where most of Kashi's fervour and activity is whirled:
in viewing a collage of bathers, florists, and boatmen,
the priests — emerging out of an art-galleries curtains.

Amidst a flurry of chants intoning to Sun and Ganges,
the most powerful one is to Shiva *'Har, Har, Mahadev'*:
as if a volley of muffled clapping for the sunrise canvas —
the auctions are bid with rituals presided by the priests.

A cool breeze caressing me I'm watching the boatman,
who deftly rows past, as if in screening a film on ghats:
each distinct in architecture, design, owing to its origin —
vying for your awareness, with every intricate detailing.

'Let's go to the centre' I goad him, 'where its deepest' —
reluctant he seems at first, to risk our boat capsizing:
yet he quietly pulls the oars, rows against the current
to float in the holy middle flow, as if to heal my soul.

At a quarter past seven, Ganges glowing with sunlight
gives my face translucence, a prenuptial facial would:
As skin potions, diets, fairness masks and beauticians —
can they supersede the benefits of soul's renaissance!

We rowed towards the sun to Kashi's opposite bank,
but I kept my eyes riveted towards the receding shore:
each ghat lent a distinctive charm as facets of past do —
retreating in slides from my recall — distilling wisdom.

　　　　Shuvashree Chowdhury

The end of a paid hour in solitude and introspection,
my past life is a beautiful series of distant experiences:
I return to the juncture I had commenced my journey —
to pave my spiritual path — regain my lost individuality.

The Lord Summoned Me

Three adorned priests, held beside us the red bucket,
filled till the brim with milk procured for our *darshan* —
we poured in obeisance — on a highly guarded Shivling
of the famed Kashi Vishwanath temple's deep sanctum.

We sought Shiva's blessings from a low brass barricade —
the presiding temple priests graciously bestowed us with
on the Lord's behalf, in silk *dhoti's* of white and saffron:
applying *tika* on our foreheads, adorning us in garlands.

Outside the sanctum, hordes were queued for a homage,
also the grand *Saptarishi arati* to commence that evening:
With strict police supervision the queues were disciplined —
omitting which, we had been ushered into the sanctorum.

On my last visit I was barely granted a moment with God,
queuing up outside early morning for several trying hours:
today at his royal court, Lord granted a sublime encounter —
so I endorse my faith, preach to the world of his grandeur.

 Shuvashree Chowdhury

A Banarasi *Thahaka* (Laughter)

An elderly gentleman with gravitas to his name —
fit and agile, over seventy — flaunts a sturdy gait;
is much respected, but is also feared in Banaras,
for he has forthright and strict instructional ways.

These defined his professor's personality traits,
of a lifetime of upholding values and principles —
prescribed in several Hindi books to his name:
while of a reputed college, retiring as a principal.

Gaya Singh, is revered in Assi by young and old;
a staunch atheist but he has a heart of pure gold —
facilitates the poor, an auto driver acquainted me,
concluding, 'At all cost, I have to keep his word!'

We met him formally — still Gaya-ji ushered us,
showing us his Banaras, hosting several dinners:
with his deepthroated, soulful Banarasi *thahaka* —
he could not hide his good-natured demeanour.

SHANTINIKETAN

Students on the University lawns

Peach flowers gazed downwards — shyly
through the green boughs dripping lights —
fluorescent, bright, they dazzled my sight,
stringing leaves in varied hued green light.

Dashes of lavender on the crust of a tree
that tenderly canopied the peach flowers —
as if into cajoling them on to a bridal bed
that was draped with well-manicured grass.

Large clouds seeming like parental masks,
threatening to burst their shadowy shapes —
on virginal flowers making love on a lawn:
in drowning their uninhibited latent thirst.

As I stood watching this drama unfolding —
that nature had lain out for me to partake:
dazzling rays of sun as arch lights zoomed
on the bullying clouds — lining them silver.

Chasing the Sunset

The July sun was set to descend over the horizon,
to bury itself — into the red earth of Shantiniketan;
I hired a Toto to ride to the site of the river Kopai —
in its slender frame — to view the sun's immersion.

The curvy smooth road through rustic landscapes,
flanked sun's tangerine hues riding trees, harvests:
a man driving two bullocks arrested my flying sight —
as with a purpose I rein in any wayward aspirations.

Sun's orange glow raced — dividing forest from sky,
like one's intention determines failure from success:
I permitted the orange balloon to lead my direction —
keeping me racing to my goal — the Kopai at sunset.

At the bridge before my goal in line with my vision,
river Kopai looked lean as goals do on completion:
I pursued further — to stop on finding a pink temple,
where I was bestowed a sunset, that was magnificent.

 Shuvashree Chowdhury

A Feast for the Soul: Shonibarer Haat

A large clearing in the woods, amidst tall trees —
on red earth over which they stand as sentinels,
under a canopy of heavy grey cloud, so full now
they seem ready to burst — stretched translucent.

Locals from the tribal villages congregate here
revealing specialized skills over handmade craft —
on striking bead jewellery, cane, saris and kurtas
spread on straw mats over a carpet of red earth.

Under several cane canopies on raised platform —
musicians regale you with tribal, *baul* renditions;
while the couple selling potato and onion fritters
from out of sizzling oil, tantalise with tangy forms.

After indulging our senses, in leaving the clearing —
my hand clutching five earring-and-necklace sets:
clouds descend on the tiny blue and white bridge
we cross, while contentedly heading to our cottage.

Riding a Toto, we soak up exotic feels of the locale —
under thick clouds prevailing on sunset's radiance
shooting off sparks of fluorescence; I feel droplets:
in a flash the road is washed by a whip lashing rain.

Through this torrential July shower ripping my soul,
I can distinctly hear the drums as if of a tribal ballet:
beckoning me to celebrate my life with little delights —
partake in feasts for the soul — with unbridled pride.

Basking in the Painter's Vision

The oval shaped veranda — overlooked a huge garden
furnished with a set of cane chairs around a glass table,
where I sat watching the grass turn varied hues of green —
ingesting slivers of morning sunlight after the light rain.

Infusing in my tea — a view of red and pink rajnigandhas
as canopy over a string of pots of yellow, orange flowers:
A black-brown greater caucal bird alights on the wet lawn —
on moist grass, basking in soft sunlight, staring me down.

This cottage like an oyster is enclosed within a green crust,
through every window on both floors only foliage is visible:
sitting on the bed it seems as we're in a cabin in the woods —
it's green at the first-floor lounge and downstairs dining hall.

A well is behind the kitchen door, from it — Moti barks at us
after his run of the front garden with trees atop lined plants:
he appears on the back veranda — my best part of this house
with a direct vision of a wrought iron swing on the side lawn.

In dampness, over several cups of tea, watching the July rain —
before or after breakfast even lunch or dinner — however late:
I'm not yearned away from sight of sun or wind play with hail,
as if in my mind — it's a large watercolour painting in progress.

The canvas I'm immersed in here is the painter's imagination —
Ganesh Pyne, had himself drawn up this charming disposition,
for the home he'd built keeping in mind every hue on a canvas:
In this veranda he enjoyed solitary detention since its inception.

In Search of the Author's Inspiration

The red mud track I stepped on — to the right of the house,
was smooth and broad, flanked by houses spaced by groves —
over which a just risen sun dodged us trailing wings of birds,
leading to a forked road with divergent setting on either side.

My instincts turned right towards the tiny wet track, to a slum —
one on the left was too picture perfect with villas and gardens,
looking urban and implanted in the outskirts of Shantiniketan,
which was originally rustic and belonged to the tribal Santhals.

Thatched roofs with billowing smoke bestow an exotic charm —
upon a semi-circular platform of shacks over which trees guard:
around here isn't another sign of life except stray pigs and dogs
and a child with wide wonder in his eyes, roaming these tracks.

Thatched mud huts in a theatre setting, painted azure and black,
are nestled under palm trees as if in pages of early painting books —
that I'd shaded with imagination, unaware they existed in real life:
this pastoral scene should've revealed to me, as a privileged child.

I had set forth, to look for Bengali-author Sunil Ganguly's house,
but landed up in the dream world recreated in his poetry and prose
which I realised were less fictional than my unoriginal sketch works —
unlike now as poet and author of novels — I value true inspiration.

After returning to the forked road, crossing to the privileged side —
I was unable to find his house — as at seven am, few folks in sight,
amid large villas enveloped by gardens in picturesque estate-lawns:
thus, disappointed I gave up — turning back to return to our house.

A few steps before I reached our well-manicured garden homestay,
I noticed a young woman coming to the mud road — out of her gate,
and so a last time to attempt to reach my goal — I decided to ask her:
when to my bliss she knew his house — also offered to walk us there.

A brisk walk back on mud tracks and I faced his house by a pond,
with plants hiding the surname of the neglected but beautiful lodge:
I spontaneously figured now — what might have been his inspiration
to title his novel I'm translating from Bangla 'Alone and a few People'.

 Shuvashree Chowdhury

ASSORTED SPACES

An April Rain in Calcutta

Sheets of steady rain blew over the asphalt road —
trying desperately to wash away layers of charcoal,
while thunder growled like a swat of hungry lions
binging on a buffalo in the woods, below a moon.

Their roars overpowering faint streaks of lightning —
no match to feline shrieks of delight — in cavorting,
inciting ferocious winds, as a coalition of Cheetahs
to chase sheets of rain — as if a parcel of white deer —
ravenous and rapid, running to escape an ambush
cheered by roaring delight — of the lions of thunder
viewing men skirting, dribbling football at an arena;
to dodge this chilling jungle cheer through showers
and score a goal — in reaching home to loved ones.

Cars sped by urgently, as I stood gauging my plight —
they did not want to be caught up at night as I might,
under a corrugated tin shed, a car mechanics garage
that came to my relief in taking refuge from this rain:
as over my daily evening stroll — I was far from home.

Viewing the rain game with stranded men and women,
under brilliant streetlights that do not classify the sights —
as an audience for gladiators at the Roman Colosseum:
I realised that living this moment was worth every effort
to type these thoughts on my phone playing radio notes —
and paint the splendour of the event in my brain's canvas
even if I was copiously drenched to my chattering bones —
through leaking sheets of tin thrashing my insulated soul.

Flame of the Forest tree in my Courtyard

You came into my life — like a thunderstorm,
bringing an essence of rain on parched ground.

Winds of your words draped me in green hope —
causing in my soul expectant tumultuous uproar.

I stand alone — wrapped in imaginary petrichor,
expectantly waiting for the overnight downpour.

But you just hover above — as big rain clouds do,
watching in anticipation, waiting to give succour.

Draped in tangerine I am drenched in longing —
mere drizzle will not satiate flames of emotion.

So you await the sizzle rain will create on leaves
dry and scorching — to gush over me full muscle.

 Shuvashree Chowdhury

Enmeshed

He comes and goes at will
as he has an independent streak,
that will not be enmeshed
in the ball of wool, you throw at him
in red and yellow colours
of love and concern —
even if it's the biggest bowl of milk
or butter for that matter
to woo his whims,
leave alone your ability
to ground or ever possess him
and keep him as your pet.

I have named him — Dude,
as he's got style and attitude —
also a flurry tail he'll swish to curl
and with a flourish unfurl,
like it was a feather on his crown
that sets him distinctly apart
from the common feline breeds —
with his wide beckoning green eyes
that pull at your heartstrings.

He is a bundle of antics — as he rolls
at your feet, rugs, or in your bedroom —
licking himself clean off the muck
his soft fluffy coat must surely pick up,
as he goes on neighbourhood strolls
to assert his independent free will —
at times not to be seen for a week.

He will then slyly creep back in
when you've given up on ever seeing him,
slithering up on your heart that is mourning —
when you drive back home one evening:
to tug at your dormant feelings
with his soft and guilty purring —
that you cannot ignore his histrionics.

Thus, you will take him back into your heart
that's still open and waiting to get entangled —
 in his playfully sweet nothings,
just like you might have allowed
the many dandies you grew up knowing —
to play with your love and girlish instincts
that had not learned to ward off
those who play to test their desirability
by repeatedly hurting other's feelings —
brandishing a fake power and masculinity
they're far from depicting with sincerity.

                    Shuvashree Chowdhury

Speaking to the Sunset

The boats on the Hooghly — they pass me by,
I don't know where they go and why —
but I stand looking on long,
hoping they'll take me along —
to my destiny that's long drawn,
also is allusive and seemingly withholds —
my dreams — that are manifold.

All I've wanted is a meaningful life —
not merely to lavishly survive,
and thus — leave footprints behind
that may cushion and guide
hearts such as mine —
that face the burdens of life
without the strength I've imbibed,
out of the struggles and strife in my life
that ought to have been sublime —
for the blessings I've been born with.

Yet my destiny dodges me around,
even as I harness all the winds to stay afloat —
over those currents I gingerly walk
like slipping and sliding boats —
creating ripples in frames of my lifelike photos.

Like the boats I'm unable to find a steady spot
where I can anchor my searching soul —
and steadily emit the orange afterglow
of lessons and values, I've absorbed
from sunshine trainings — at corporate jobs,
also, through trying bridges of experiences
I've diligently crossed, in the prime of my life —
to give me a steady shine as my sunset years dawn,
so with a purpose — guide my path lifelong.

Autumn in Kolkata

I'm strolling the bowered pathway,
swathed in an autumn sunlight —
slinking in through tangled vines.
My face is flushed in tones of the blossoms —
caressed by a nip in the air — romancing October's
shiuli, champa, and chameli flowers.

The festivals persist unabated,
today the popular north Indian — Karvaa Chauth,
when for the longevity of their husbands —
women fast daylong — in obeisance to them
who over their lives supremely influence,
but tonight, under the full moon are summoned —
so the wives can break their daylong fasts
viewing through a sieve — the moon with their lords.

The gesture is romantic and has tradition no doubt,
but reeks of subjugation and male clout —
for only a woman fasts for the welfare of her husband,
as we women, since eternity — lead a sheltered life.
Yet on a whim want our independence and flight —
which to get — we blame every man in sight
but aren't ready to give up on the benefits —
of the male-dominated society we live in,
for who are we to deny a heritage we've imbibed!

  Shuvashree Chowdhury

But last month, we have worshipped in Bengal —
the strength, of a woman in its potent form,
Goddess Durga and her four children;
by rejoicing in her slaying of the demons —
most of poverty and suppression,
that lives here have turned into a dungeon:
bestowing upon all transient gaiety and fun —
even if it's only week-long every year
that the city of Kolkata comes to a halt —
leaving us forlorn when the goddess is gone.

But we sooth our emotional fall
by cushioning it with another serial festival —
celebrating goddess Lakshmi and her carrier — owl,
in a dedicated puja — though venerated a week back
along with her mother Durga, and siblings —
for Lakshmi is the goddess of wealth and luck
that we wish to cajole into our homes and lives.

As Dhanteras, Kali Puja and Diwali draw near,
the nip in the late October air now much dearer —
the aroma of shiuli permeating my senses
as the days are getting shorter —
the mornings more dewy and quieter,
and fog slowly pervading the night air
that make me value homeliness I'm steeped in:
but motivates me to step out of my mental bower
to project my inherent strength of being a woman.

Colours of Diwali Light

The light dazzles my eyes,
as the sparks emitted —
come in every conceivable
shape, colour and size.
They fill up the staid autumn sky —
setting my heart aflutter
like all those butterflies — daylong
hovering around garden paths,
sucking nectar from flowers —
of every colour and form
that are now in full bloom
amidst the houses and barns —
of my childhood fantasies,
from all the classic novels
I'd keep my head buried in,
that would transport me to another world —
to hide from the reality of my loneliness.

These Diwali shards of brilliant light —
now ignite my mind's eye,
setting my thoughts racing wild
to when I was a child of nine
and sorely afraid of the dark.
So that, I'd close my eyes and run
to the light switch boards on the far wall
of my boarding school's dormitory,
if I came up to my locker out of time —
feeling my way with my hands,
panicking but managing not to fall —
in playing blind-man's-buff with my fears.

                    Shuvashree Chowdhury

Later, I'd extricate myself from self-doubts
so I couldn't lose my sense of self again —
in the flurry of adult life — when at work
I'd fight for my self-esteem, and rights —
not act as a victim in trying circumstances.
Then, when life would turn into dark alleys of men —
trying to exploit — overpower me with their influence,
throwing me overboard many a times:
but always delivering me from my own torch —
strong beams of logical reasoning and brilliance
to guide my confident and unique strides.

Keeping the Lamp Aglow

It's the morning after Diwali,
I'm sitting out on my balcony at home —
viewing the line-up of all the burnt out *diyas*
that tenderly glowed through last night —
vibrant in a multi-coloured sequence
with tiny light bulbs and slim candles,
amidst the champa and chameli flowers —
emanating distinctive aromatic scents
enveloping me in nostalgic self-assurance —
from reminiscences — of candles lit in youthful bliss.

A white ball slowly comes into my view —
it must be the sun I convince myself
as it's adorned in a glowing — orange-ring of hope,
rising over our railing that's wrapped in shrubs.
The fresh sun, blushes in shades of tangerine —
climbing out from cut-paper decorated terraces,
dissipating its passionate glow far and wide
to raise the sleeping world into a latent new morn,
where yet — only a lone pigeon daintily struts
over the slim waves of an old asbestos rooftop.

I look down at my half-finished cup of green tea —
atop the tray — in green and white vine print,
when the sudden gust of a chilly breeze
sends delightful shivers down my spine —
as there's anticipation in approaching winter sunsets,
leading to Christmas and New Year moonlight dusks.

   Shuvashree Chowdhury

The crows crowing, pigeons in hoards descend —
over a rooftop with glamorous Diwali decorations,
bringing me back to the present moment
when there's peace, joy and contentment,
as that's what love and hope do to determination
to live pursuing dreams — with a vision and mission,
without worrying about what your destiny might unfold —
so long as you bear the torch of satisfaction lifelong,
that your heart's not yet — and never going cold!

Rekindling Memory Slides

I'm sitting at my desk this morning
when the sky turns a deep leaden grey,
the clouds become dense as smoke —
impregnated they are, with August rain.

It's been rather humid the past days
and I've bodily been in a lethargic state,
but my soul's wondering amidst the clouds —
my heart and mind in total disarray now.

The streaks of light amidst the thick haze
dazzle my eyes — as steady rain descends,
mango leaves in varied green shades bristle —
as if water spluttering over a charcoal kiln.

Slender trees at my window sensuously swish,
as palm hand fans held by housewives' slim wrists —
they fan white and red bordered sari frames with,
rekindling my Bengali childhood memory slides.

  Shuvashree Chowdhury

Creative Delight

This morning, in Kolkata's Central Park,
I walked the rain drenched paths
swanked by lush green grass —
over which varied tall trees
sheltered a multitude
of gallant flowers and plants.

The eastern sun, in gearing up
to display it's splendour and might
over the torrential rain and lightning
that dazzled the August night —
it peeked at me rhythmically
through branches astride:
as if a Chhau dancer showcasing his art —
decked in a brilliant gold ensemble,
grabbing my awaking mind's eye.

White birds with sure yellow feet
hopped over puddle-drowned grass,
shoving their yellow beaks
into crevices and cracks
of fallen tree trunks floating as rafts.

Yet around these sights and
sounds of chirping that abound,
morning walkers rushed past —
indifferent to nature's practiced dance:
oblivious to a painting with words or a brush,
forming in my mind's eye of its own accord.

It's a new day that's washed clean now —
of yesterday's dusty thought tracks,
awaiting my pristine mind now
to collate all these numerous slides —
to form a kaleidoscope of creative delight.

Shuvashree Chowdhury

Don't write Me off

I might be past my prime of youth —
but see, I'm aging gracefully:
don't write me off — I'm old wine,
my words, a rehearsed symphony.

The sparkle in my traversed eyes
has withstood life's numerous storms,
as for my smile — it has braved treacheries
and yet can inspire many a curiosity.

I might as well be losing physical agility,
but my mind's a pliant willow tree:
its osiers now weave thoughtful word baskets —
training youth, its timber long shaped cricket bats.

I have never listened to anyone over my heart
as people preach out of their experiences of failure:
for I prefer to be guided by stories of success —
not let fear, but intuition with hope, be my leader.

So, don't write me off, until you taste my word elixirs —
of curiosity, a resilience that keeps me motivated:
my heart as an airbag, it braces rejections and failures,
for I've nurtured a banyan sapling of self-esteem.

On a Full Moon, in Chennai

I'm now chasing remnants of a setting sun —
its orange light guiding my path;
with distant sounds of the chugging train —
on its beaten tracks I fix my gaze
to catch glimpses of the moon,
arising from the depths of the earth
as a backdrop of light for dancing clouds.

On my walk, I had followed the silver gleam
of the full moon — that led me enticingly,
past sharp bends, into deserted lanes —
to peer into bungalows that gleamed charmingly:
emitting flower essences from under windows
curtained in prints of seasonal-bloom upholstery.

Fancy cars lined handsome T-Nagar bungalows,
as back from work — owners crouched indoors
over their smartphones, with air-cons whirring;
television channel debates drowning
barks of large well-bred dogs inside grill gates —
who unlike humans, could not resist
the tenderness of the full moon's romancing.

                    Shuvashree Chowdhury

The Present Moment is all I Have

On a beautiful Sunday morning —
the first one this March,
I sat down as usual at my desk at home
to type like I do — on my keypad,
with my steaming teacup.

Barely had I taken from it a sip,
when a woman barged in
looking ghastly and petrified —
her eyes piercing into mine:
'Your Ma's fallen', she announced.

A moment to process her words,
recalling Ma was out on her usual walk —
my world came crashing to my feet,
gut freezing first and then my heart —
in recall of the familiar feeling of Baba's loss.

I grabbed a shirt, and pants from my wardrobe,
for in my night gown I could not go to a morgue —
as that's where I envisioned Ma — if hit by a car,
in manoeuvring at seventy-seven — the aggressive traffic
that now wouldn't let me find and gather her carcass.

I blindly ran on the street like a possessed woman
for I didn't know exactly where I was headed,
as I desperately pleaded with God — to give me a moment
to gather Ma up, even if she breathed her last in my arms:
I couldn't bear to imagine her dying on the road, unclaimed!

To my shock I found her in a car, at the end of my street —
a kindly man, to rush her to medical aid, had seated her in.
Ma looked at me with glazed eyes as if it was her final goodbye —
the way Baba had the last time — her blood gushing in a stream,
spurting out of the *dupatta* she held pressed to her nose.

I got into the back of the car, held her firmly to the front seat —
my heart pounding like being thumped by wild bears,
as I repeatedly intoned: 'Ma you're going to be fine, don't fear',
while I directed the man at the wheels to rush to a hospital —
one I mentally sprinted towards — with my positive thinking might.

We reached an emergency unit, before she might black out —
where with impatience I watched them execute procedures,
as for hours — the reputed hospital ran a battery of tests
starting with an injection to stop the bleeding — then a CT scan,
till announcing 'she will be fine'— they handed her to my care.

Its forty-two hours, since a disaster that might have taken Ma away —
leaving me emotionally numb as in the aftermath of a hurricane,
with Ma recuperating in hospital to be monitored, fix repercussions:
I'm back tonight at my desk to leave this poignant written trail —
with a missive, to live every moment — as this moment is your life.

                         Shuvashree Chowdhury

A Village in Bengal

That morning at nine, we set out on a lengthy drive,
crossing expressways, hotels, and airport to our right.
 The flyovers we crossed were modern and manifold —
above high rises and abodes — the airplanes groaned.

Bally bridge we traversed over the Hooghly's high tide,
Belur Math and the Dakshineswar temple to our right:
across lush harvests was a rustic and picturesque sight,
water bodies rippling under wide expanses of blue sky.

Altering an erroneous course — despite of google maps,
on village tracks to the red and white Rajbari's ramparts:
the vintage edifice was imposing, its office cosy and small —
huge palm hand fan on its wall, green door in relic form.

The courtyard, with a Radha-Madhav temple led to stairs,
to high-ceiling rooms lodging zamindars of 14 generations:
our cosy room and foyer, gave an old worldly regal charm —
view of garden, lotus pond, poultry pen, wood-chessboard.

A gondhoraj sharbat heralded the traditional Bengali meal
at a dining hall across our room, facing the inner courtyard:
served on *kasha* plates with half a dozen bowls of vegetables,
there was dal, *luchi*, rice, curried eggs, chicken, and mutton.

After a siesta, imparted its history, we went on a guided tour
of a palatial home that has retained its Zamindari splendour,
with unique furnished rooms, each of the kin had resided in —
depicting the last chain of its residents' lives, named therein.

Past a foliage to a walled lake — house ladies had bathed in,
we walked up to a cow shed, its occupants now gallivanting
amidst lines of cottages that flaunted deer, rabbits, and fowl —
all sprinting around, making a cacophony of unique sounds.

We were taken on a brisk stroll of this palatial country estate,
also, outside it — to a temple on the opposite side of the road:
back inside to public offices, dance hall, rooms full of antiques —
we were shown the splendour of well-maintained royal spaces.

Over a visit of two sprawling kite-flying terraces during sunset —
from where was audible a medley of musical accompaniments
of the priest's *arati* at the *alpana* bedecked well-lighted temple:
we descended to partake in it — seek Lord Krishna's miracles.

After few games of ludo, snakes and ladders, also badminton,
over *masala chai*, snacking on vegetable *pakoras* in the garden;
under a cemented canopy, we watched a drizzle turning to rain —
then relished a classic Bengali dinner with rice, curried mutton.

At seven next morning — I wandered out of our imperial fortress,
originally built in 1766 by the Borgee Maratha's — titled 'Kundan':
to sneak a view of the village, Itachuna that was renamed 'Kundu'
by this family who had built here — a school, college, and hospital.

I walked awed by lines of well-to-do cottages flanking clean roads,
pretty with manicured gardens — waking up late to a winter's sun:
a maze of paths amid tiny ponds in which flocks of ducks paddled —
but the exotic mud huts stood up with elan, vying for my attention.

After cups of Darjeeling tea following walks in the Rajbari's garden,
we ate an elaborate breakfast of *luchi* with typical Bengali garnishes:
then took on the village roads — to drive back into urban civilization,
to duplicitous lives where there's no reprieve from class distinctions!

                    Shuvashree Chowdhury

The Scents of a River

I am standing by the pier dressed in aquamarine blue,
swathed in the setting sun's tangerine hues —
watching the birds glide past on their homeward flight
over the hull of a mermaid shaped cruise ship
that I'm to board — in a few minutes.

The wood-planked walkway I cross
with purposeful slow strides —
the wind caressing my face, neck and mind
to an awakened sense of reflective delight —
in keenness of a river cruise over the Ganges
 I've diligently organized — to end the three-day festival
for poets, who have congregated from over the world —
to recite their poetry in Kolkata — India's cultural capital.

After we have all settled on the top deck of the ship —
aptly named Matsyakanya — the mermaid:
it seductively drops its sturdy moors, setting sail
into the musky river odour — pervading my senses,
and stirring up my restless and anxious emotions.
The mermaid shaped hulk enticing my imaginative mind —
into picturing the river as the cosy arms of night
beckoning the mermaid into her boudoir —
to be seduced by the gallant moon craving her bosom.

We set off the slated poetry readings once seated,
after we've recouped from the sublime environment —
our minds moulded into a soulful mood that's essential:
with soft ripples of the river drawing us into its groove,
as it's forging ahead fervently to meet the Bay of Bengal.
The vessel, creating a soft beam of light awakens our minds,
that we may appreciate the beauty of multilingual verses
to coerce now — through the sea of our own thoughts.

When we crossed under the Howrah bridge —
we took an interval from the ongoing poetry readings,
as I looked up and articulated a wish under my breath
in the age-old belief — it would be divinely ordained.
Just then, liveried waiters came around with platters —
serving delectable *kebabs* and fish fingers
that tasted divine with mint *chutney* and tartar sauce —
both in the menu to appease palates, bridge the east-west gap.
Thus, tempting our value for words, sincerity of our thoughts —
assessing if we are poets defenceless to worldly enticements
that tend to muddy the profundity of our opinions!

A lively jazz band now performs as we cruise along —
as series of ghats come alive, with twinkling lights
beckoning us to disembark — for glimpses of their soul.
So that we may romance them with a profusion of words —
once we return to our own faraway shores:
as poets, are we not crusaders of isolated inner voices,
who take it upon ourselves — to uncover private worlds!

There is now an aura of candescence around Belur Math —
after we cross the Dakhineshwar Kali temple ghat,
that wraps us in its eclectic, mystic charm
in arousing pictorial minds — poets are endowed with,
though we now tend to rely on cell phone photographs
over the astute lenses our mind's eyes are gifted with!

The dinner of Biryani — with several accompaniments,
also, number of continental selections for international poets —
has just been served on silver-plated buffet salvers
that now reflect lights of the embankments we traverse.
Just like shores we cross in our lives varied sojourns
reflect the perceptions forming our dishes of words,
refined as we are in choices of word-condiments, as gourmets —
for as poets we perceive profoundly with all our senses,
much sharper and more sensitised than most people.

                       Shuvashree Chowdhury

There is a divine caramel custard for dessert,
also vanilla ice-cream drizzled with chocolate sauce and nuts —
to cool, and soothe our spice ignited sensory nerves.
So that, we may return to our personal worlds satiated —
or we might consider our evening's experience inane,
before we convert this sublimity into words and phrases
to leave sincere and optimistic imprints on Kolkata —
not only as an ailing and poverty stricken 'City of Joy'.

The night chill of the river breeze beckons us to return,
to the pavilion of commencement of our excursion —
from the fading lights of a series of ghats now left behind,
that will recede into the remote wilderness of our minds —
perhaps never to surface, even till we are dead and buried
or cremated — ashes sprinkled in some edge of a river as Ganges.
May our souls rest in peace then over our life's word choices —
to uphold values despite resistances and fear of social ostracization,
thus, avoid regret at culmination of our life-cruise's cryptic end!

An Uphill Drive on Hairpin Bends

Early this morning we'd taken the flight —
arriving at Coimbatore to commence our drive
to the town of tea plantations — Valparai,
which I'd only recently learned about —
even though living in Chenna:
and then planned this weekend trip —
from the April heat — for some reprieve.

After an hour's drive in low-traffic before eight —
through the business city's arterial highway,
we arrived at Pollachi — a small, clean district
where we were to begin our ascend at foothills.
After relishing the finest *chutneys*, with *idlis* and *vadais*,
and the most aromatic filter coffee I've ever had yet —
it revived our sleep-lacking minds to now appreciate
the pristine beauty we were to absorb on the way.

Blue-sky draped mountains came into sight
as if sea-waves of varying heights —
over which, green trees — an alluring essence adorned,
as at a high-society event perfumes of ladies disperse —
while in their gaiety, around tall men they dance.
The trees as if men — on whose branched-arms,
varied birds delightfully alight for a while,
before they fly away to form patterns in a dazzling sky
that's just been washed clean by the light drizzle —
and now the birds are sitting out to dry
in the early sun's soft warm light — dripping in
through the window, draping me in Cashmere delight.

As we deftly hasten on the slim, winding hill path —
at every turn of the slow and tedious climb,
as on the landings of the staircase of life —
there's a prize we're thoughtfully awarded

                    Shuvashree Chowdhury

of an amazingly picturesque, unique sight:
unravelled to us by God — who has bestowed
upon those willing to trod an unforeseen, untold road —
trusting him to shower benevolence and goodwill
to elevate us to a higher and grander plane,
thus discover and fulfil our life's ultimate purpose.

On each hairpin turn that we deftly took —
up the steep but sturdy hill road,
a stone slab imbedded into the earth
marked the number we crossed —
out of the forty turns we'd have to traverse.
At each turn, as we got off to get better sights,
I felt a reinvigorated confidence to surge ahead in life —
for failures, hurdles, rejections, hatred and criticism,
each is a distinctly marked turnpike in life's ascent
to be spanned until a garden of successful delight —
from where we can assess the world with our own vision
without being prejudged and quizzed of our intentions —
on whether the path we chose will enhance your life.

At the end of the fortieth hairpin bend
akin to one's fortieth year of life,
was a thick forest, so beautifully scented —
it felt like entering an aromatic uplifting spa
in which, playing the recorded strums of a guitar,
varied insects loudly screeched a joyous hallelujah
over their short life with little purpose, unlike us —
who in this wide life, don't find cause for gratefulness
that we may pass onto subsequent generations —
to live for a cause, and to find a joyous purpose.

This forest abounds in a variety of animals —
tigers, deers, leopards and elephants,
among them — there are also giant squirrels,
and yet insects among the titans mark their presence
in the buzzing voices God has gifted them,

without feeling thwarted by their minuscule existence.
Outside this enlightening and refreshing forest
we come onto smooth road flanked by tea plantations —
through whose tiered landscape there's mountains
that stare back at us — through tall trees that arrest rain,
to ensure bountiful and quality tea and coffee harvests.
As Varpalai is not a tourist but commercial terminus —
plantation staffs are gainfully employed, clothed, and fed
by six owners of the fifty-six estates generating wealth.

Next morning from my bed, under a quilt —
I hear the siren, summoning workers sharp at six,
above the sounds of assertive cawing,
a few melodious — also unidentifiable chirping,
with a neighbourhood hen clucking, rooster crowing.
In the distance I see planter's cottages lined on low hills —
cradled in their midst — a wide span of multi-layered green;
all of it shrouded in thick mist playing hide and seek,
snuggling me in a deluge of joyous and cosy chill.

                     Shuvashree Chowdhury

Freedom in Confinement

A mistake I made in life
that I cannot now rectify,
yet I can still live a meaningful life —
even if it's in prison confines.
As I have the gift of art —
of paintings and handiwork,
to guide my wasted life
with hope and light.

I once had much love,
support of home and hearth —
with family and friends to count on.
Also, a life well laid out,
with dreams and aspirations
to guide my youthful path.
But then, choices I made in life —
circumstances guiding my stride,
proved me guilty of a crime
where my destiny was maligned.
Landing me in prison walls,
that took people I loved off my sight —
for no one cared if I was still alive,
even if mere breathing is hardly a life!

Yet life showed me a spark of light
in the darkness of my confines —
a kind lady through her NGO — Rakshak,
brought in an oil lamp of hope.
Out of painting and craft lessons, she evoked
in all of us men and women —
a renewed will to live and be known
for our skills — as a beacon of hope,
not merely for mistakes we've committed in life —
thus, burying us alive in our dark confines,
from where not even a sun or moon is visible.

Now look at these rays of coloured light
that my dark world has illumined,
through this exhibition
at the Indian Museum in Kolkata,
filling me with pride and appreciation
that my paintings are fetching
from generous people and organisations,
who love art in the preservation of heritage —
to reinforce Kolkata's culture — I was born in
and am now passionate in upholding.
To enable a life of beauty and satisfaction
I had never dreamed of for myself —
nor had my parents and friends,
not even for my children had I imagined —
who were ashamed of my existence!

     Shuvashree Chowdhury

Space in the Time of Caronavirus

We all seek it; we all own it —
yet we are all lonely in it
as, who really knows
how much is too much —
or for that matter who knows
how much space is too little!

I need to call you — to come over,
to check if you have time for my visit.
When all I'm really doing, is
hiding in a soulless internet vacuum,
till there comes a point in time
when you will no longer seek me.
For the space between us
has grown further than the horizon
I view — looking out to sea,
from where you seem so remote
I cannot even invite you to tea.

As a child when I went out visiting —
Baba, Ma, my sister and I;
we called upon friends and family
who welcomed us graciously
as there wasn't a need for —
ringing of remote bells of the telephone
to awaken love that was reciprocal.
As affection — wasn't constricted in form,
into spaces of isolation we are now in —
for haven't we beckoned distance for long,
in begging for Space — unwittingly!

Acquainted with Isolation

I've been acquainted, with being on my own
even when all around there was commotion,
on play fields at lunch times, in locker rooms
I have been alone with myself — my thoughts.

In my mind there's always constant dialogue
so I don't need any external noise stimulants;
or the company of people hurling arguments,
trying to gain each other's banal affirmations.

Yet I enjoy a sincere one on one conversation,
to listen to your soul as you do not your own —
for you're not connected with your own core
in trying to mask from me or from your soul!

Isolation has been a choice I have made in life,
yet try me, I'm deeply connected to this world:
for noisy, cluttered minds sink with judgement —
in looking out to sea for lifeboats of validation.

My reactions to painful experiences in this life
have been as if its milk boiling over with froth:
even if — bubbling over from my various facets
I don't jump out, so on stoves of pain it settles.

In trying to withstand life's difficult situations
till I can withstand the searing heat no longer:
I calm down even through my streaming tears
to become immune to this virus for a lifetime.

There are times, I have cooled my saucepan —
then someone recreates tough circumstances
to put me back on the heat of a burning stove:
but I'll sit through if it's worth the relationship.

 Shuvashree Chowdhury

After a point with close people I lose patience —
with those I do not care to waste my emotions:
I cut off their gasoline supply into my calm life,
to power off negativity I disconnect their stove.

Company of people I seek only out of a choice,
it gives me self-assured strength, and resilience:
for without the ability to tune inward to oneself,
loneliness will come by — visiting you a lifetime.

Coronavirus lockdown is a medication for those,
who fear isolation in fear they might be all alone:
if they stand up for their opposed self-conviction —
to create a formidable strength from deep within.

A Double Distress

Sheets of rain flew around in the howling wind,
haphazardly thrashing bungalows and buildings;
not a bird in sight, as mango, neem trees rustled
in the sounds of charcoal sizzling on a brick kiln.

A mid-May heat sizzled melting in frenzied rain
pouring on parched houses, gardens, and streets —
as if struck by a series of matchsticks of lightning
on emotionally ignitable homes coping isolation.

The thunder growled angrily on green mangoes
frolicking with their crowns now a ripening gold:
as if children going berserk — to return to school,
to curriculums they won't dread, after lockdown.

Our stray kitten Minni, was excited this morning,
as animals connect with nature unlike us humans:
in fear she brought in her new-born, but first time —
we shooed her mistaking it for a rat in her mouth.

But Minni wasn't deterred as she dodged around
till we built her kitten — the carpeted carton house,
as even for a kitten safety of her child is foremost
for she perceived, oncoming of cyclone Amphan.

Evening sky is grey, with streaks of light flashing
on stringy coconut-tree leaves, dancing a cabaret —
atop the terraces we've watched the sun set gaily
in pink, tangerine, last two months of lockdown.

Nature reminds us of its power in unique ways
but where do we heed its whistle-blower tactics,
till we're pinned down to this complex distress —
to risk death, in a jobless lockdown or out of it.

　　　　Shuvashree Chowdhury

Love Died, last Night

She didn't live — Love didn't survive,
despite all the attention, we lavished
after her mother brought her inside,
to save her from — cyclone Amphan.

Three days, Minni hovered around
watching one of her kittens from far,
as she had entrusted her to our care
after she could not save the first one.

Minni herself barely six months old —
learned to oblige, lying on her back
when Love was positioned over her
to demonstrate, assist her to suckle.

Love, lay in the carton shelter all day
without ability to move let alone play —
while Minni licked, squatting on her,
sure, her baby was safe in our charge.

Three days as we watched constantly —
minding his every turn Love squealed
giving us hope she would soon crawl,
but abruptly — Love breathed her last.

Minni afar — must have heard her cry,
recognising in it, Love's final goodbye —
for she hovered near us, but not Love
who lay lifeless — a week's life enough!

Minni even had a meal, her child dead —
 after she waited to assess this situation,
then lay down — away to come to terms
with her loss, and its emotional impact.

With my persistence Minni drew near
but only to meow goodbye, feebly lick
Love, she had braved from the floods:
now how could she dare look at dead!

There must be nothing heart-rending
than a mother who can't even mourn
the death of new-borns — even foetus,
in saving from this treacherous world!

                    Shuvashree Chowdhury

My Feline Family

Tinni, was the first one to arrive
amongst the three kitten siblings —
spotted black, beige, over white,
with wide eyes — a visual delight.

These kittens, were months old,
when they walked into our door
after the Persian tomcat — Dude,
for whom, ours is second home.

Tinni, Minni and Rinni grew up
and were shortly joined by Jason
the tomcat — who now wooed all,
impregnating them — one by one.

Minni, the first one to give birth,
at six months — was a poor mom:
her instincts were not yet formed —
couldn't save her two new-borns.

Tinni, wasn't she smart after all,
so gave birth right on our couch
then suckled, licked for warmth —
grabbing attention, with aplomb.

We made Tinni a carton home
as a week back we had for Minni:
Tinni squatting, guards her kitten —
she might have felt Minni mourn.

Dude, views his nieces, detached,
but Jason gingerly prowls around:
our feline family in the lockdown
only delight in Whiskas cat meals.

The cats bring solace in isolation
but, are free to go out and prowl:
aren't carriers of deadly covid-19
so return home to our neighbours.

It's a lesson, innocents are spared
from being carriers of coronavirus —
thrashing humanity onto its knees:
as nature — avenges its exploitation.

                    Shuvashree Chowdhury

Harbinger of Hope

Azure is the dusky sky,
with streaks of fairy lights
riding cobalt blue waves —
floating up in a sea of haze.

A basket-moon cruising tonight
to contain tomorrow's full moon —
that is a harbinger of Hope
to shower the tired Earth
and draw it out of its cocoon —
the coronavirus relegated it to

The Tarot Card Reading

Rain is about to pour down in torrents,
as clouds overhead weigh down full strength
over the muddy Ganges that's calm as night —
stirring emotions in lockdown — bound tight.

A medley of coloured boats near the shore —
as if cards displayed on a Tarot reader's desk;
from which she'll shuffle a deck at a time
to pull out cards, interpreting mysteries divine.

It's three months, yet the coronavirus raves —
making us dance to its fluid psychedelic waves
that keeps us distressed, in a trance of anxiety,
but nature stares at us serene, as the Hooghly.

The boats are ready and waiting to be rowed
but not many souls are in the mood for Hope —
to care to make a wish from under the bridge
that now looks gaunt and so powerlessly still.

Young couples in strewing the riverbanks
on Saturday night dates — are still well masked,
and cautious to maintain social distancing —
Love in the time of Coronavirus is daunting.

 Shuvashree Chowdhury

Destiny Delayed, or is it Denied

The sun strained to look at me
just a few more moments —
through window grills of thickets,
with its tired bleary eyes.

As it slowly slipped into a coma
under a blanket of clouds,
forcing it into the deathly folds
of the gaunt Hooghly at night —
that has lost its immunity now
after four months of lockdown.

It hasn't eradicated coronavirus,
which still spreading like wildfire —
is burning up economic life:
yet again testing the resilience
of the 'City of Joy' Kolkata,
a land that history has bellied —
cyclone Amphan mocking its plight!

Yet with arms full of sunny warmth —
it has always taken in destiny's denied
since the times of the two partitions,
or for that matter, neighbourhood strife!

A Spiritual Sojourn: My Renaissance

"Death must be so beautiful. To lie in the soft brown earth, with the grasses waving above one's head, and listen to silence. To have no yesterday, and no to-morrow. To forget time, to forget life, to be at peace."

— Oscar Wilde, The Canterville Ghost

The nurse woke me up at seven this morning,
though — to my phone alarm I'd already arisen:
so I might shower, dress, and be ready by 9 am —
to be trolleyed to the theatre for the operation.

Mildly sedated the night before so I sleep well —
I am fresh and mindful of my every movement:
Though not a drop can I drink — since waking,
not a bite did I intake last night, after it was ten.

It's a bright sunny morning outside my window
yet there isn't a spring in my heart, step or voice:
A solemn calm pervades my soul prepared to die —
like in films — the convicts readying to be hanged.

I brushed, looking outside a wall-to-wall window —
saw a painting of a tree by a multicoloured house:
Two nurses walked in-and-out readying my room,
laying out a starched white backless surgery gown.

I showered breathing slowly, conscious of my form —
as bathing a dead woman before her funeral sojourn:
Drying my hair, I shrouded in a white hospital gown,
to lie in view of a sky that'd be, even when I'm gone.

Wheeled on a bed, down the corridor and into a lift,
conscious of each turn I shut my eyes looking within:
Would my soul grief in not returning on these aisles?
I realise there's no regret — I've made peace with life!

 Shuvashree Chowdhury

Outside an OT they dial my mother, sister, two friends;
with each on video chats — I realise how detached I am:
Like it didn't matter if I were never to see anyone again —
as I've always given all I had to give to each relationship.

Shielded in a sky-blue blanket, they stripped my gown —
the writer in me shut eyes after a mindful look around:
Then the only sensation I was aware of was biting cold,
like I had sat up on my death bed on a thick slab of ice.

I realized now, I wasn't going to die, my mind is strong —
shutting off from life was my soul's defence mechanism:
test of my spirituality, having lived every moment of life,
the fighter in me would survive — I have unfinished tasks.

Anaesthesia overriding — took over the baton of my life,
passing it on to the expert surgeon and team — to resolve:
first thing I profess is a searing pain — in floating up to life;
swathed in soft sunlight — in a baby pink robe I'm reborn.

*"Life and death appeared to me ideal bounds, which I should first break through,
and pour a" torrent of light into our dark world."*

— Mary Shelley

AN ARTISTS RETREAT

The Red Thread of Fate

The Red Thread of Fate is an East Asian belief originating from Japanese and Chinese mythology. It is commonly thought of as an invisible red cord tied around the little fingers, or around the ankles of those that are destined to meet one another in a certain situation — as they are their 'true love'. The two people connected by the red thread are destined lovers, regardless of place, time, or circumstances. This magical cord may stretch or tangle, but never break. This myth is like the Western concept of soulmate or a destined partner.

With a bottle of red wine, I rang your doorbell,
when you answered it looking into my keen eyes —
anticipation was ripe from years we have not met
since personal turmoil stormed both of our lives.

Our meetings so far were intimate but far flung
after we met at the social event seven years back:
though we bonded rich over our commonalities —
life's hurts fudged — mutual trust and judgements.

A fine red thread kept our little fingers connected
over time, continents, and our chaotic professions,
to throw us back on love's stage after a year's exile —
that I may passionately fight to save your reputation.

Our souls embraced long now beyond a quick hug,
even as we exchanged gifts, you gave me a silk scarf:
I'd chosen essentials you'll need for your official trip —
wherein destiny brought us together after a long time.

The skyline dazzled us as I sat down by the window,
taking a few sips of wine, then looked into your eyes:
a theatre became set to where our chemistry leads us —
into each other's arms — kissing away the lost years.

We'd first connected on a winter's evening long ago,
with long chats over homemade dinner and red wine —
yet beer by the sea over a barbeque truly bonded us
into taking the leap of faith to plan a getaway together.

The full moon and stars etched on the glass window —
warmly lit the stage for a drama we were to perform:
as the gallant hoardings, stately minarets, and towers
lent our theatre's soliloquies an entrancing backdrop.

In an opening scene you checked if stage was well lit,
I went about ensuring the props on the set were firm:
our dialogues inspired by deep emotion got muffled
as fluidity of steps of our dance-drama got profound.

Synchronisation of steps and fluid body movements
in a dance — comes with regular, repetitive rehearsals:
but two people intuitively gauge each-other's longings
if the sole intention is the other's need and fulfilment.

Lying panting for breath cradled in each other's arms,
the spotlight focuses on our profound act centre stage —
in taking the audience up to a frenzied emotional state,
they need to descend — before they applaud our dance.

In the last act our full-course lively dinner scene plays
as in the restaurant set — we savour the Bengali cuisine:
the magical chord connecting us by now — is so elastic,
it's red colour deep with trust, has turned nonabrasive!

        Shuvashree Chowdhury

In Search of meaningful Colour'

"Our desire lends the colours of the rainbow to the mere mists and vapours of life"
— Rabindranath Tagore, Stray Birds Fireflies & Other Poems

We drove out leaving behind the festival of Holi
in search of colours to drench our souls with —
a crocheted quilt of green embraced our sojourn,
cajoling us into lush green rural harvest fields.

Roads had lean traffic but our eagerness was thick,
as at crossroads we stopped to take directions
to our exclusive duplex house by the river Ganges —
in it we'll drench in privacy's enchanting colours.

Google maps coaxed us smoothly all the way
till an imposing complex's gate tried our patience —
in checking our reservations beyond endurance,
even so — the drive up was misleading, until arrival.

A thrill in getting away — but an anxiety prevailed
till settled in after lunch served by a caretaker —
overlooking the swimming pool that ran at length,
past row houses facing each other till the river.

On a siesta you undraped me — off silk-lavender,
every bit of my skin crooning to you in rupture —
as you coloured me deep purple and fuchsia pink
then deftly absorbed the colours into your skin.

With a clear midday blue sky streaking upon us
we drenched in all of fires' conceivable tones:
as our skins glistened red, blue, orange, and green
in lovemaking, colours erupting from our soul.

We blushed a rose-pink from prolonged doting,
reflecting the glow of sun's steady descension —
infusing into our hearts that for long was missing,
a fierce embrace of our soul's ardent affection.

You colour me as no one else, seeking redressal —
that I more than readily bestow on your lips,
in seeking to find my own sensibilities fulfilment,
so I'm appeased — you also know to partake in.

Our bodies drenched in colours of our desires —
we're swathed in its overpowering emotions:
contentedly fulfilled, cradled in each other's arms
we finally let the blanket of sleep bind us in.

Holi this year has been most special for us so far —
as it coloured us in a love — all encompassing:
In every life, a deep meaningful love is necessitated,
to paint our visions — creative expressions with.

    Shuvashree Chowdhury

As Sun Sets in Ganga's Lap

It's five in the evening and I must promptly step out,
as the sunset over the Ganges beckons me now:
I've showered, spritzed Eternity, worn white and pink —
but you don't notice and refuse to accompany me.

I walk the poolside avenue — down a temple parapet,
past a carpark flanking lights that are knee-height:
then into a gate, the garden of lotus ponds embraces —
as lotuses peek coyly as brides by Ganges's side.

To bless the '*swayamvar*' of lotuses by courtly boats,
the sun now wears on its tangerine — royal cloak:
a metallic mesh — tulle, veils the lotuses from cruisers,
as their demure look hides their burning desires.

Close to the edge I walk — keeping Ganges to my left,
trail her contours as lovers trace the other's body —
craving tongues needing no respite from discovering,
each crevice lovingly possessed of mind and body.

The sun by now is a passionate orange ball of fire,
with desire consuming sights — so far colliding:
a point when Sun could not grow fiercer in its glow —
he slid into Ganges's lap, into her lover's thighs.

I walk no further — mind drenched in sunset ecstasy
from infatuated lovemaking of Sun with Ganges —
on whose breast's birds soar as boats trail her belly:
Sun drops into Ganges's folds — the day is buried.

God Kissed my Hand

I'm sitting with you on the banks of the Ganges,
looking into the horizon that's a patchwork —
of colours and emotions harmoniously blending
into sunset jaunts, of our four-day excursion.

The sun is a flaming ball of tangerine this evening,
illuminating our visages in megawatts of love:
sitting centrifugal to two power transmission towers —
built in Bengal, among the tallest in the world.

A crematorium by a Shiva temple — we just passed,
reminding us we're well crossed in life's paths:
so must savour each moment of joy life now imparts —
leave imprints of love, that our death will flout.

A lone stray dog strolls up purposefully to my side,
almost kisses my fingers craving a loving touch —
as if a harbinger of the message of strength from God:
distressed I may be — but am sheathed in his love.

 Shuvashree Chowdhury

The *Jatra* of Life

Children, men, and women, came rushing to a stage —
from where — the new *jatra* had just commenced:
they stood around in circular form on the mud road,
amidst houses, series of brick kilns, and tiny stores.

A traditional theatre form of East and West Bengal,
the *jatra* is performed by avid travelling troupes:
for this drama, we had barely arrived in all spectacle —
by a sheer stroke of luck, thrust upon this village.

On our sojourn drenched in a sunset over Ganges,
we drove out to this village outside our realm —
where we've come far, to get away from our worlds
to recharge emotional batteries in imagination.

A broad clearing over the mud track — as we halted
to brushstroke our senses in photographic rays —
the sun laid out its net as if on a catch of mackerel,
in blue green it spread its essence into darkness.

The road now narrowed as we drove on in silence —
on bumpy, curvy mud roads dusk descended:
soot chimneys from brick kilns lined our river trail,
as kilns gradually shut their large campus gates.

Glittering fairy lights of a wedding showed up afar,
daring us on — as beacons of human existence:
a trail squashed by river and walls, closed in on us —
yet with your moral strength I perilously edged.

Cheery children, and youth, looked at me curiously —
'See, see, a woman is driving' — they chorused:
as I recognised the dead end of a quest undertaken,
and, 'all that glitters is not gold' was thus proven.

On my left — road steeply plunged into the Ganges,
the right encroached on shops, house estates:
Anxiety grabbed me by the bones, still I shoved on —
fortitude from our love bolstering the car's fall.

Villagers who hadn't seen such a dramatic spectacle —
cheered, encouraged, guided me to manoeuvre:
while to resist the car slipping as handbrakes resisted,
you got off to push — to get us safely back on track.

The simplicity, gutsy moral fibre of Bengal's rural folk —
boosted my strength, and the car back on safe track:
just as love's emotional crane uplifts my life-boat's hull
to a secure waterline, keeping my confidence afloat.

     Shuvashree Chowdhury

Happy Hour Margaritas & Mojitos

Over dinner at the restaurant, at Happy Hour,
we were jubilant to say the least on Margaritas:
at a price for two we got four, bought two more —
Cointreau, Tequila, lime juice — in perfect mix.

Dislodging slices of lemon from the glasses rim,
tasting salt off it we gently squeezed lime juice in —
ingredients shaken well with ice, tingled tongues
flavoured by prawns and lamb, also fish n chips.

Our conversation's light with drizzles of the blues —
to thaw frozen hearts doesn't take many cocktails,
as it swirls your soul where the past is a hurricane:
like lava hurt melts, overflowing a brim of reason.

Night after, we return for a Happy Hour advantage —
they run out of Cointreau — to our disappointment,
but our wells of melancholy we've not yet exhausted:
to instil happiness we'll opt for eight Mojitos instead.

Our Piano Recital

Nestled in a house by the backwaters of Ganges,
on a mystical getaway to alleviate our sore hearts —
we're at home in a solitary retreat that is sublime
with a backdrop of silence, dense trees and birds.

The house faces an unserviceable landscape pool,
the television channels are non-receptive and cold;
a cleaning lady and male caretaker at our disposal —
offer their services if it's dictated yet remain aloof.

With firm hands you adjust our living room settings —
streamline sofas, table, satisfy architectural stirrings:
rinse crockery, cutlery, organise them in symmetry,
line up Green and Darjeeling tea, red wine, whisky.

There's much I'd say to end your defensive forays —
appreciate you in creative, endearing, soulful ways:
You are still reeling, from past experiences of pain,
so, I bid my time to earn your trust, get you to dare.

Our books, phones, laptops neatly by our bedsides,
bathrooms displaying lotions, oils we use, varied soaps —
we do not violate each other's moods or private spaces:
order I seek in my life is in tandem with your elegance.

Yet with bashful fingers you massage love up my spine,
from your mind's page holder playing passionate notes —
inciting every key in my body to come alive as in choir:
eager to play upon your piano's keys my frenzied notes.

Your shyness quivers with the intensity of your passion —
yet fears it will succumb to the anxiety of performance,
as you do not trust — our feelings ride a tandem bicycle:
thus, imprudent to risk vulnerability of our soul's union.

            Shuvashree Chowdhury

It's the depth of my love that makes me so perceptive,
as I play over your keys to feel music fill out your soul:
I risk vulnerability to let you see my raw nerve endings —
it's in communicating we'll decipher each other's notes.

My fulfilment in allowing you play on all my secret keys,
is so that we might create a melody with our own theme:
to soak in the potency of love I'll risk heart's destruction —
for happiness, as in bungee or scuba diving, faith is vital.

Pieces of Shadow: on Jasmine scented Canvas

The tips of my fingers, tingle with jasmine —
its sensual essence coursing my imagination;
yet its fragrance isn't driving my awakenings,
but my tracings on art-paper over your spine.

The jasmine almost universally loved, evokes
memories of summer evenings, gentle breezes:
in uplifting one's spirit it relieves the physique,
dissolves emotional barriers, growing intimacy.

I pour this oil over my palms to anoint you with
but it's my fingertips bringing your painting alive —
they deftly glide in and out your curves, crevices
as I crave to touch you in carving out your profile.

My fingers aflame with yearning of deep feelings
in outlining your skin that glows as if molten wax —
its dripping drop by drop onto my longing palms,
guiding my imagination in tracing your silhouette.

Black paint dipped in oil — I trace your thick hair,
also, the distinct eyebrows you lift at me curiously:
in soft strokes I brush the jovial deep brown eyes,
then my lip-brush passionately devours your lips.

Silk-fingered brushes chase lips down your torso
as my tongue outlines each brown tipped contour,
for bearings it might have on your mind's leanings —
in bringing you alive on my portrait for all to view.

I hope, yours doesn't end like my other paintings,
for the well of my love's imagination is yet so deep —
filled with longing that's got you on this canvas now
at this artist's retreat of which only you have a key.

    Shuvashree Chowdhury

It is an ethereal experience I've never had before,
to feel the potency of two creative minds on fire —
as I take the lead to finding inroads on art-paper,
with burning fingers, paint shy craving curvatures.

I imagine you painting me in your unique colours —
only your artist's mind-palette is capable to blend:
though its all focused on your mind's photo vision,
your hands are shy in taking my imagination's lead.

It's in painting you I make sensuous love to you,
for in my creative mind's eyes both are the same:
as they equally require sincere erotic involvement —
only in according pleasure, you derive fulfilment.

I sense the depth of your overpowering emotions —
as I'm painting my fingers feel you burst into life:
still you're afraid of vulnerability, haven't the trust
you'll be loved — childlike soul flaunting a parasol.

I dream up a child with our personal endeavours,
as we erotically prepared dough for the sculptural —
to infuse the figurine with both our creative senses
but impregnate it with a fearless heart — resilience.

We're making love on solo canvases to each other,
on two paintings, with passionate hues and flavours:
jasmine oil's only a base to mix our erotic fervours —
as the body has fewer inhibitions — than our minds!

My Spiritual Alcove

"When a man finds that it is his destiny to suffer, he will have to accept his suffering as his task; his single and unique task. He will have to acknowledge the fact that even in suffering he is unique and alone in the universe. No one can relieve him of his suffering or suffer in his place. His unique opportunity lies in the way in which he bears his burden."

— Victor E. Frankl, 'Man's Search for Meaning'

I love the cosy haven this alcove now provides —
under a window, cushions on mattress recline:
curtains drawn upon the bedside — give respite
from my restlessness — also prying curious eyes.

Lounging at this villa's poolside since predawn,
at a first-floor window alcove — on our sojourn:
I watch as birds in flight begin their day in song —
drapes of darkness on world's theatre withdraw.

I view the sky's stage crack up into a soft dawn —
as it were the cool breeze goading its meltdown:
like a poached egg — sunny side now cracks up,
spilling into its white that is coagulated in form.

It's a whirring wind on the backwaters of Ganges
that's flowing sideways behind a landscaped pool:
it reminds me to put the electric kettle on to heat,
as tea may soothe my unease and bring on sleep.

Over honey green-tea I contemplate on the book —
'Man's Search for Meaning', by Victor E. Frankl:
A bevy of storms crashing on me since childhood,
yet like the rock of Gibraltar I've faced life's wrath.

          Shuvashree Chowdhury

For if I lose faith in my future it's surely doomed,
along with losing my well-fortified spiritual mould:
allowing myself to crumble at any crisis that arrives —
subjecting myself to a mental and physical decline.

Sunlight, by now has enlightened my mind's eye,
it's warmth — now percolates over the eastern sky:
in life's storms, I view an objective deep meaning
as it's guided by purpose — in my case my writing.

My life's stage now well lit, mind calm I lie down,
with soft sun's rays lighting up my face, also limbs:
Despite of it I now fall asleep, for my mind is still —
emotions with a clear perspective, cannot wring it.

Contented from Life's voyage

"Night's darkness is a bag that bursts with the gold of the dawn."
— Rabindranath Tagore, 'Stray Birds Fireflies & Other Poems'

I'm looking out of the large, draped window,
with my mug of honey-lemon green tea —
at a green forest barricading timid backwaters
of the mighty Ganges's Bengali tributary.

It's past four am, I've been jolted out of sleep —
my mind's intense inside my relaxed frame:
even after three days of relaxation in harmony
in the lap of luxury near river and greenery.

A cool March breeze caresses the pool and me,
both filled gradually until recently, after Holi:
in gallons of love, chlorinated water, respectively —
for people, souls to bathe in my intellectuality.

The boat hulk lies sideways, with its hips raised,
contented from life's voyage through thickets —
calm, contended as a woman — in love's embrace
after a passionate bout of soulful lovemaking.

The woman and boat lie in seductive naked glory,
exhausted and spent — but seemingly happy:
after love has washed them over on their side-hips —
sprawling on their beds of green embroidery.

I stroll around the poolside my mind still leaden —
it's past six am, a March sun's vaguely lighting,
washing the boat's belly it streams the lake blithely
to creep up the window, wrap up lover's nudity.

                    Shuvashree Chowdhury

In the soft glow of the sun through a quilt of love —
their forms are shaded in obscurity but visible,
yet both woman and boat hulk are still lonesome:
they're emotionally single — in this wide world.

The End